D0897986

THE LETTERS OF
MARY RUSSELL MITFORD

THE LETTERS OF
MARY RUSSELL MITFORD

SELECTED

WITH AN INTRODUCTION BY

R. BRIMLEY JOHNSON

KENNIKAT PRESS
Port Washington, N. Y./London

THE LETTERS OF MARY RUSSELL MITFORD

First published in 1925
Reissued in 1972 by Kennikat Press
Library of Congress Catalog Card No: 76-160763
ISBN 0-8046-1583-7

Manufactured by Taylor Publishing Company   Dallas, Texas

PREFACE

MISS MITFORD'S *Letters* can be found in (1) *The Life of Mary Russell Mitford*, related in a selection from her letters to her friends. Edited by the Rev. A. G. L'Estrange. 3 vols. Second, revised edition, 1870 : (2) *Letters of Mary Russell Mitford.* Second Series, edited by Henry Chorley, 2 vols., 1872 : (3) *The Friendships of Mary Russell Mitford*, as recorded in letters from her literary correspondents. Edited by the Rev. A. G. L'Estrange. 2 vols., 1882 [containing, also, a fair number of her own letters *to* literary friends] : (4) *Memoirs and Letters of Charles Boner*, by R. M. Kettle, 1871 [with over two hundred pages of letters from M. R. M. to Boner] : (5) *Mary Russell Mitford. Correspondence with Charles Boner and John Ruskin.* Edited by Elizabeth Lee, 1914 [a few, not very interesting, letters to Ruskin and his father, with a reprint of (4)]. Some further letters were printed by Mrs. Browning, and others appear —incidentally—in biographies of the period.

This selection does not present an autobiography but a personality ; the letters being chosen for their individual interest or their style, and given complete. No arrangement but the chronological would be satisfactory, as few are written throughout on one topic or in one mood.

The Introduction, again, aims more at characterization than criticism ; the intention of the whole book being to reflect all aspects of a remarkable woman—whose name and work are known by repute.

R. B. J.

CONTENTS

CONTENTS

THE LETTERS OF
MARY RUSSELL MITFORD

INTRODUCTION

MARY RUSSELL MITFORD, 1787–1855

" MAMMA says," writes Miss Mitford to her irresponsible father, " *the great art of letter-writing is to construct an epistle without one possible subject.* And truly, if such be the fact, no two people have a better opportunity of improving in this way than those who have the honour of sending you a sheet full of nothings. Indeed, my dearest love, upon a careful revision of our letters, I do not suppose that upon an average they would be found to contain one piece of intelligence a week."

Elsewhere, in a slightly more serious mood, she describes her " theory respecting letter-writing " :

" *Rien n'est beau que le vrai ; le vrai seul est aimable*, is my motto ; and translating ' le vrai,' rather according to the spirit than the letter, by ' the natural,' I believe that you will agree with me. According to my theory, letters should assimilate to the higher style of conversation, without the snip-snap of fashionable dialogue, and with more of the simple transcripts of natural feeling than the usage of good society would authorize. Playfulness is preferable to wit, and grace infinitely more desirable than precision. A little egotism, too, must be admitted; without it, a letter would stiffen into a treatise, and a billet assume ' the form and pressure ' of an essay. . . .

" A little character, a little description, a little narrative, a little criticism, a very little sentiment, and a great deal of playfulness."

To say that Miss Mitford *practised* all that she preached would be to contradict her " theory " itself ; for spontaneity, if not expressly named, is clearly essential to a " natural " style in letter-writing.

But she possessed, by instinct, the nature and the gifts which led her frequently to express herself in the manner which she theoretically approved. She may, indeed, fill her sheet with " nothings " ; but in the artistic sense she " improves " the occasion—with playful grace. There is " art " in her egotism. She does, as a rule, write a " good " letter, in which, however subconsciously, style plays its part, life is a little dramatized, and thought is given to the tastes or interests of the person addressed.

Their easy frankness creates personality, giving life to the trivial matter ; and, as it happens, Miss Mitford has something casually intimate to reveal about a number of the great men and women whom every one must desire to have known. Her own views or impressions *are* her own ; decided,

independent, and therefore valuable to us : whether
or not critically sound. She reflects, of course,
the outlook and atmosphere of her period ; but we,
who can only know the artist through his art, are
always eager enough to hear *How it strikes a con-
temporary*.

Women-writers, of their pioneer century, from
Fanny Burney to George Eliot, brought naturalness
into literature : and where their journals or letters
have also come down to us, reflect the times, as
few men save Boswell had the power or the inclination to attempt.

And Miss Mitford, unlike Jane Austen or
Charlotte Brontë, saw a good deal of literary
society, read widely, and was familiar with the
critics : never failing to criticize on her own
account. " We moved last Tuesday," she says on
Sept. 27, 1851, " a terrible job. There were four
tons of books ! ! ! " and the great majority of her
letters include some reference to a new author
she has discovered or just met.

They are addressed, moreover, to artists and
men who wrote books or cared greatly for writers :
her father, with all his faults, was a cultured en-
thusiast and at home among big people. She was
accustomed to " the higher style of conversation."

Yet, strictly speaking, there were no *realists* in
those days : no one " took up his pen " without an

eye for dramatic effect. Miss Mitford, we must
not forget, refers to " the ' art ' of letter-writing "
as an " opportunity for improving " ; and the
intention is even more plainly marked in explaining
her own classic volume—*Our Village*.

" You, as a great landscape painter " [she is
addressing Sir William Elford], " know that in
painting a favourite scene you do a little embellish,
and can't help it ; you avail yourself of happy
accidents of atmosphere, and if anything be ugly,
you strike it out, or if anything be wanting, you
put it in. . . . And as you, in common with all
sensible people, like light reading, I say again that
you will like it." The modernist, certainly, does
not " improve " life after this fashion, either in
books or letters ; but the tradition was long
upheld.

" Of course," she admits, " I shall copy as closely
as I can Nature and Miss Austen . . . I am afraid
with more of sentiment and less of humour " ; but
a good deal is " left out " even in *Mansfield Park*
and *Persuasion*. On the other hand, Miss Mitford
claims as " her chief advantage in novel-writing,
that she will be able to go higher and lower than
Miss Austen " ; and the class-mixture enlivens
her letters.

They are, in fact, far more racy than *Our Village*,
and at their best deserve to be at least as well

known. The combination of a literary flavour and critical power, of a keen love for animal or inanimate nature and certain forms of sport, with shrewd sympathies and strong family affection, produces a rare charm.

Her " sweet dandy," indeed, " had an idea that she was blue-ish " ; but her " confession " was not addressed to *him* : " I write merely for remuneration ; and I would rather scrub floors, if I could get as much by that healthier, more respectable, and more feminine employment."

There is some convention, and a good deal of bitter self-pity, in so drastic an utterance of contempt for artistic ambitions ; since " to get money "— and pay the debts continually incurred by her father —" was so much her duty, that that consciousness took away at once all the mock modesty of authorship."

But, in fact, she had been almost a prodigy in her youth ; the " Poems " and " Plays " are rather " blue " ; and, on the other hand, there is no mistaking her genuine pride in the " matchless Elia's " praise of *Our Village* that " nothing so fresh and characteristic had appeared for a long while." In reality, she was well aware that to create a " beautiful race of dandies " brought keener pleasure to the artist than the most adept handling of a scrubbing-brush could confer on the housewife :

" Great as my admiration has always been of the mechanical inventions of this age, I know nothing that has given me so high an idea of the power of machinery—not the Portsmouth Block-houses or the new Mint—as that perfection of mechanism by which those ribs are endued in these stays."

Miss Mitford, indeed, sometimes allowed her tongue, or her pen, to run away with her, regardless of her own motto on truth, " le vrai seul est aimable " ; and was never afraid of being frankly inconsistent :

" I have discovered," she once remarked with glee, " that our great favourite, Miss Austen, is my countrywoman ; that mamma knew all her family very intimately ; and that she herself is an old maid (I beg her pardon—I mean a young lady) with whom mamma before her marriage was acquainted. Mamma says that she was then the prettiest, silliest, most affected, husband-hunting butterfly she ever remembers ; and a friend of mine, who visits her now, says that she has stiffened into the most perpendicular, precise, taciturn piece of ' single blessedness ' that ever existed, and that till *Pride and Prejudice* showed what a precious gem was hidden in that unbending case, she was no more regarded in society than a poker or a fire-screen, or any other thin upright piece of wood or iron that fills its corner in peace and quietness. The case is very different now ; she is still a poker, but a poker of whom every one is afraid."

Miss Mitford, you see, was in society, and like
" most writers, a good-humoured chatterer "—not
a wit ; but her *amende honorable* shows real feeling.
On Sept. 13, 1817, she " had not heard of Miss
Austen's death. What a terrible loss ! Are you
quite sure that it is our Miss Austen ? " And it
appears that Miss Mitford's " friend " had " family
connections " uncomfortably associated with the
Austens, in some matter of an " entail " ; which no
doubt helped Mrs. Bennet to hate the egregious
Collins.

Miss Mitford, it should be remarked, is usually
kindly and generous in judgment—to those whom
she personally meets : young Mr. Ruskin, Charles
Kingsley, or Wordsworth. Like Mrs. Browning,
and so many of that generation, her enthusiasm for
Napoleon III. is unbounded ; and we must hesitate
as to the sources of information inspiring her
statement that

" The Prince and the Queen are now so much
afraid of the result of that folly the Grand Exhibition (1851), that they will only go up to town for
state balls and drawing rooms, and continue to
reside at Windsor. Already the park is a scene of
tremendous disorder. Think what it will be when
all the mob of foreigners and our own artizans
shall be added to the rogues and pickpockets of
London ! Besides which, after having built the
trees in they will infallibly be cut down, and I
believe everybody is agreed in wishing that it

could have been all swept away and things replaced as they were."

This, certainly, is not the view with which our parents have generally sought to impress us.

Mary Russell Mitford was an only child, born at Alresford, Hampshire, on the 16th of December, 1787 ; in childhood hugely spoiled by the fond parent she was later doomed in turn to spoil, no less fondly, until his death.

Letter-writing, it seems, had been a family gift from the days of George II. ; for her maternal grandfather, Dr. Richard Russell of Christ Church, when a widower of forty-eight, composed the following " elegant epistle " to win a second bride —with " a certain sum of money " and heiress to fifteen hundred pounds :

MADAM,

Though I hate lying, I am, you know, a little given to story-telling, which shall serve as a preface to what follows, being taken out of a book, whose author was no less a man than a cardinal and prime minister of France.

" A certain gentleman, called Themistus, happened into the company of a young lady, whose sight struck him with great admiration. Celimene (for that was the lady's name) being but of a very mean fortune, though of an extraordinary beauty, Themistus, who had immense riches, made many serious reflections upon this sudden and violent engagement. But, fearing lest his passion, which he felt so violent in its beginning, should in the end

lead him to the satisfying his desires to the prejudice
of his fortune, he resolved to banish from his soul
so dangerous a tenderness. He opposed it therefore all he could. But, finding he could not
presently overcome it, he called in a sentiment of
glory to the assistance of his reason. He had the
resolution to part from what he loved, and to go
a volunteer into the army. But he returned thence
more amorous than he went, and visited his mistress
with greater joy and· a stronger desire. Then,
blaming himself for his weakness, he made a second
effort, and undertook a second voyage, which was
to Italy. He would try, it seems, whether pleasure
and diversions would appease those inquietudes,
which perils and fatigues could not allay. But the
carnival of Venice was as little conducive to that
purpose as the siege of Breda ; for he appeared at
his return more ardent and passionate than ever.
My dear Philemon (said he, speaking to his friend),
*I lead a wretched life ; I cannot forget Celimene;
I have her always in my thoughts, and I see her continually before my eyes with all her charms.   In short*,
(added he, and this was his saying), *I must marry
her that I may cease to love her*. Accordingly he
did marry her ; and fifteen days of marriage changed
his violent and tumultous love into a sweet and
delightful friendship.''
   I have told you, Madam, this French story, that
I might have an opportunity of observing to you,
that the consideration of fortune is of no weight
with a real lover ; that a true love is not to be
diverted by any sort of engagements from its
beloved object ; and that the most violent and
tumultuous passion will in a reasonable mind soon
terminate in that greatest of earthly blessings, a
most '' sweet and delightful friendship.''

That you are not in the circumstances of Celimene—I mean as to fortune—is, I own, a pleasure
to me, because I am not in those of Themistus.
But my passion for you, you may assure yourself,
is no less real than was that of Themistus for
Celimene, though I have not the opportunity of
showing it in the same light, and to the same
advantage, which he had.

If I was master of the world, I would lay it at
your feet. As I am only owner of a small part of
it, I offer you the whole of what I have—and am

My dear Miss Dickers,

Yours most unfeignedly,

R. RUSSELL.

ASH, *August* 31, 1743.

It was, no doubt, just such " most violent and
tumultuous passion " by which Mr. Collins was
" carried away " towards Elizabeth and Charlotte.

The reverend gentleman himself possessed " a
good private fortune " ; to which Miss Mitford's
mother became the heiress, in " the golden age of
five per cent." We are told that " *in addition to
these attractions*, she had been carefully educated ;
and to the ordinary accomplishments of gentle-
women, had united no slight acquaintance with
the authors of Greece and Rome." It was, perhaps,
" the plainness of the face—the prominent eyes and
teeth—the very bad complexion, scarcely redeemed
by a kind and cheerful expression," which induced
her to throw away herself and, as it proved, her
fortune upon the handsome young doctor, ten

years her junior, Dr. George Mitford, " the younger son of a younger brother of Mitford of Bertram Castle in Northumberland ! " who, " in middle life, lost the lithe grace of the Apollo and expanded into the larger proportions of the Bacchus " ; but at eighty, still kept the " remains of extraordinary personal beauty."

Her money, and other sums, passed into his hands, but soon fell out again ; from his " careless manner of holding " them. For " he was not only reck-lessly extravagant, but addicted to high play."

Whether this medical Adonis really possessed some almost magical fascination, or whether his womenfolk were exceptionally forgiving and self-deceived, we cannot, of course, determine ; but the fact remains that his wife and daughter always admired and loved the man, holding no sacrifice too dear for his sake.

" Of one thing I am certain," writes Miss Mitford, when she was old enough to know better, " that the world does not contain so proud, so happy, or so fond a daughter. I would not ex-change my father, even though we toiled together for our daily bread, for any man on earth, though he could pour all the gold of Peru into my lap. Whilst we are together, we never can be wretched ; and when all our debts are paid, we shall be happy."

He paraded the child, as an infant prodigy,

before his grand relations ; but lost his temper at the slightest personal discomfort or inconvenience, and proved " incapable of sacrificing the slightest inclination of his own for the welfare of his wife, or even of his daughter."

Miss Mitford, indeed, never writes to him as a responsible parent. He is always her " dearest darling," her " dear runaway," and " best beloved," her " sweet Tod," or her " gitimate son and air." At twenty-four she " implores him " to " tell her the full extent of his embarrassments," that they may " confine themselves to humbler hopes and expectations," retaining " only their *real* property." That the poor man may not " give way to depression," she " longs to see him, to pet him, and love him, and tell him pretty stories of ' Marmion,' and show him pretty glowworms ! "

Thirty years later we see how deeply the struggle had eaten into her heart, how seriously she herself regarded the disgrace of debt :

" Yes, my dearest, my mother's fortune was large, my father's good, legacies from both sides, a twenty thousand pound prize in the lottery—all have vanished. My uncle's estates, his wife's, his father's and mother's (a fine old place called Old Wall, in Westmoreland ; she—my grandmother— was a Graham ' of the Netherby clan ')—all have disappeared ; so that I, the only child amongst six or seven good fortunes (for my mother—herself

an only child—inherited an even splendid inheritance), have been, during the better part of my life,
struggling with actual difficulty ; and, if I should
live long enough, shall probably die in a workhouse
—content so to die if preserved from the far bitterer
misery of seeing my dear, dear father want his
accustomed comforts ;—content, ay happy, if that
far deeper wretchedness be spared."

Her " consolation " is generous indeed. It was
a great grief, leaving the " dear old country house "
for a little cottage in Three Mile Cross, but :

" I could not, I think, so quietly have borne the
change to a town. And yet I don't know ; there
is a blessed principle of conformity in human
nature, and I should have fallen into the artist-
society of London, where clever and cultivated
men and intelligent women, after a day spent in
their various pursuits, meet at night . . . without
fuss or ceremony, or dress or régale of any sort—
calling in quietly, without preparation, at each
other's houses between seven and eight o'clock,
and staying till ten, or going, with equal disregard
of appearance, to the theatre."

Such sober reflections, however, were far from
her mind at that " very early age," when she was
" perched on the breakfast-table," that she might
read aloud, " from the Whig newspapers, to
admiring guests . . . a puny child, appearing
younger than she was, and gifted with an affluence
of curls, which made her look as if she were twin
sister to her own great doll " This breakfast

room, in her first home, was " a lofty and spacious
apartment, literally lined with books, which, with
its Turkey carpet, its glowing fire, its sofas and
easy chairs, seemed, what indeed it was, a very
nest of English comfort. The windows opened
on a large old-fashioned garden, full of old-
fashioned flowers, stocks, honeysuckles, and pinks."

It is scarcely necessary to mention that the house
had been Mrs. Mitford's, before her marriage ; they
sold it within nine years ; and we next hear of the
little newspaper reader " on the Surrey side of
Blackfriars Bridge " ; where the doctor had " found
a refuge from his creditors within the rules of the
King's Bench."

That was about 1795 ; and relief came from a
strange quarter. Still a spoiled child, Mary was
taken one morning to " the lottery office," made
her choice at once of the number 2224, and won
twenty thousand pounds ! Dr. Mitford, with equal
celerity and no more foresight, found " a new red-
brick house " at Reading, in which to enjoy life
" with his phaeton, his spaniels, and his greyhounds " ; trusting " the number of trumps at
whist " for the maintenance of his good fortune.

Miss Mitford was now ten, and " decidedly fat.
Her face, of which the expression was kind, gentle,
and intelligent, ought to have been handsome, for
the features were all separately good and like her

father's, but from some almost imperceptible dis-
proportion, and the total change of colouring, the
beauty had evanesced." So she remained through
life, " never common-looking," always loved and
admired, but undeniably plain.

As a schoolgirl her " thirst for information " was
always " eager "; and she carried the day against
her parents for the addition of that " perfectly
unnecessary " Latin, to her studies in " French,
Italian, history, geography, astronomy, music,
singing, and drawing." She " danced in the ballets
and acted in the plays "—by Hannah More. As
each year drew to a close, " her little spirits were
all abroad to obtain the prize, sometimes hoping,
sometimes desponding "; and " the dear little
rogue " felt the keenest " gratification in puzzling
her instructors "; catching them out more than
once.

Meanwhile the doctor had purchased a farm at
Grasely, three miles out of Reading; and, always
" a fidget," proceeded at once to pull down the
dilapidated but romantic Elizabethan " country
gentleman's residence," and erect the " uniform "
Bertram House; so named after the castle of his
Northumbrian forbears.

Here Miss Mitford came home in 1802, aged
fifteen; her schooling complete, and ready enough
for the " Race Ball " and other " gaieties of the

neighbourhood." She had already discovered that Goldsmith's *Animated Nature* was " quite a lady's natural history, and extremely entertaining . . . free from technical terms, generally the greatest objection to books of that kind " ; and had become not only a voracious, but a critical, reader. She could not admire the *Æneid* so much as the *Iliad*, found Dryden " careless, heavier reading than Pope, too fond of triplets and Alexandrines." For five years a catalogue kept by Mrs. Mitford reveals her reading, an average of fifty-five volumes per thirty-one days ! for exercise " going out with her mother in the green chariot."

It was from here that Miss Mitford obtained her first sight of London ; " was extravagant enough to give half a guinea for a dress skirt . . . had the happiness of seeing Mr. Fox mount his horse . . . listened with transport to the elegant Mr. Whit-bread . . . in her very convenient black gown " ; visited the theatres, the picture-galleries, and Westminster Hall. In the same year, 1806, Dr. Mitford conceived the idea of satisfying the double vanity of showing off his " clever and accomplished daughter " in the Ancestral Halls, and of impressing *her* with their magnificence. They " went the first two stages on the box of the barouche," and " sat down sixty-five to dinner." Though " generally thought very proud, . . . a most

lovely woman who dresses with particular elegance," the " charming Duchess " proved more
attentive to Miss Mitford than " Lord Charles "
had ever known her " to any young person before."
She is anxious Papa should not know that one
morning " three different people called before we
were up, and four more before we had done breakfast." In the evenings she " read aloud to the
ladies, and the gentlemen played billiards, and
occasionally visited us." It was " Lord Charles's
friseur " who " cut *her* hair " ; though he was " by
occupation a joiner, and actually attended with an
apron covered with glue and a rule in hand instead
of scissors." Unlike Catherine Morland, however,
she was exceedingly disappointed by the appearance
of a modern " Abbey "—" the occasional residence
of a man with an income of a hundred and ten
thousand pounds. It has on the outside an appearance of a manufactory and the inside conveys the
exact idea of an inn."

No doubt Miss Mitford enjoyed the tour ;
although, for a time, her pleasure was cruelly
interrupted by the eccentric selfishness of Dr. Mitford, who had suddenly rushed back to Reading
for an election, broken off all his engagements in
Northumberland, and left her to find her way home
as best she could. Friends, however, were kindly
sympathetic ; and, in the end, the " dear runaway "

was persuaded to rejoin his daughter and conduct
her properly to Bertram House.

By this time Miss Mitford had begun to write
verses for occasional publication ;—" I could forgive their being trifles—but, alas ! they are heavy
trifles—lumpish, short, and thick and squab as
their luckless writer herself." She now regarded
herself, and was regarded by her friends, as what
we should consider an amateur author. Dr.
Mitford was often absent in town, to win, or lose,
money at " Graham's " and even at " inferior
clubs " where—as his daughter once warned him
—he had to " deal with slippery gentlemen." She
herself, though always delighting in the country,
was not averse to London visits, where she would
go " first to Bedlam, then to St. James's Street to
see the Court people " ; or to a " most elegant
supper, upwards of three hundred people, every
delicacy of the season in profusion, chalked floors
and Grecian lamps ; in superb apartments lined
with beautiful exotics," where she " danced till
five " in the morning : her " partners uncommonly
pleasant, but still heart-whole."

A volume of *Miscellaneous Poems*, kindly received
but of no great merit, was ready in 1810 ; and the
same year brought about an introduction to the
landscape painter, Sir William Elford, to whom a
large number of her most interesting letters were

written for many years ; a valued and lifelong
friend, at this time " verging upon sixty-four."

The old gentleman " coaxed me into a correspondence, which was of no small use to me, as
giving me a command of my pen, and the habit of
arranging and expressing my thoughts. *He always
said that none of my writings were so pleasant as
those letters.*"

But the gossips began to talk, and Miss Mitford
declared to a friend :

> " I shall not marry Sir William Elford, for which
> there is a very good reason : the aforesaid Sir
> William having no sort of desire to marry me ;
> neither shall I marry anybody. I know myself
> well enough to be sure that if any man were so
> foolish as to wish such a thing, and I were foolish
> enough to answer ' yes,' yet a timely fit of wisdom
> (caprice some might call it) would come upon me,
> and I should run away from the church door. . . .
> He is the kindest, cleverest, warmest-hearted man
> in the world, perfect in everything but not being
> in love with me."

There was, naturally, a tone of deference to a
distinguished senior ; but Miss Mitford is out-
spoken and frankly independent on any topic, and
never " wraps up " her tastes or opinions. The
letters contain much shrewd criticism of the
English classics and new books, of life and men ;
interspersed with anecdotes, humorous or pathetic,

intimate gossip, and lively pictures of country scenes or her numerous four-legged pets.

She makes free confession of all her hopes or fears concerning the poems—published or contemplated—and the attempted dramas ; which now filled a large part of her thoughts, and were fairly well known, especially in America. But she had evidently not yet discovered the only field in which her work was destined to achieve distinction.

It was some nine years before the appearance of *Our Village*, that she thus laments her inability to write prose :

" I have been teased by booksellers and managers, and infinitely more by papa, for a novel and a play ; but, alas !—far worse off than the worthy citizen of Molière, who had spoken prose all his life without knowing it—I have been obliged to refuse because I can only write in rhyme. My prose—when I take pains, is stiffer than Kemble's acting, or an old maid's person, or Pope's letters, or a maypole— when I do not, it is the indescribable farrago which has at this moment the honour of saluting your eyes.

" This is really very provoking, because I once— ages ago—wrote four or five chapters of a novel, which were tolerably lively and entertaining, and would have passed very well in the herd, had they not been so dreadfully deficient in polish and elegance. They had no more grace than a dancing bear ; so I threw them into the fire forthwith, and have never since adventured out of the leading-strings of metre. Now it so happens that of all other qualities this unattainable one of elegance is that which I most admire and would rather possess than any other in the whole catalogue of literary merits. I would give a whole pound of fancy (and fancy weighs light), for one ounce of polish (and polish weighs heavy). To be tall, pale, thin, to have dark eyes and write gracefully in prose is my ambition ; and when I am tall, and pale, and thin, and have dark eyes, then, and not till then, will my prose be graceful."

She never became " tall, pale, thin " ; but she *did* learn to write prose ; and, as she once remarked, " you are aware, I hope, that all clever people begin by writing bad poems."

We learn, meanwhile, that " the Wordsworths never dine ; they hate such doings ; when they are hungry they go to the cupboard and eat " ; or we are entertained by drastic comment upon Mr. Perry of the *Morning Chronicle* ; who " hired " Hazlitt, " as you hire your footman," without " the slightest suspicion that he had a man of genius in his pay, nor the most remote perception of the merit of the writing. . . . I well remember the doleful visage with which he used to contemplate the long column of criticism and how he used to execrate ' the d—d fellow's d—d stuff ' for filling up so much of the paper in the very height of the advertisement season."

She earnestly thanks God " for the constitutional

buoyancy of spirits, the aptness to hope, the will to
be happy, which I inherit from my father."

Yet the close of their life at Bertram House was
at hand ; and no one but Dr. Mitford was to blame.
No word of criticism or complaint was ever uttered
by his daughter ; but we can now understand the
feverish desire to write—poems, or plays, or articles
—anything that will bring in cash ; and the almost
greedy concern with which she treats the question
of pecuniary reward.   Mrs. Mitford was a cheerful
and " managing " housewife ; accepting without a
murmur the continual " reductions in the establishment," which had begun as early as 1808.   But
when she is driven to begging her husband for a
" one pound note by return of post " to obtain coal
or bread, it is obvious that " ruin was eventually
completed."

The women declare that he " was always cheated
and ill-used, wronged and over-reached " ; and,
like all gamblers, he is known to have indulged in
numerous speculative investments, on which the
inevitable losses were very probably owing as much
to the rascality of others as to his own folly.   But
all was due to his selfish and reckless love of play.

By 1820 they were at last compelled to exchange
house and land for " a cottage—no, not a cottage—
it does not deserve the name—a messuage or tene-
ment, such as a little farmer who had made twelve

or fourteen hundred pounds might retire to when he left off business to live on means." With her unswerving courage, Miss Mitford describes the change in a few quiet words ; but the cruel suffering and profound regret are plainly enough revealed.

" I was, as you may imagine, a little grieved to leave the spot where I had passed so many happy years. The trees, and fields, and sunny hedge-rows, however little distinguished by picturesque beauty, were to me as old friends. Women have more of this natural feeling than the stronger sex ; they are creatures of home and habit, and ill brook transplanting."

But it had to be : Three Miles Cross, " only a mile nearer Reading in a little village street situate on the turnpike road . . . stood ready to receive " her ; and she must learn " to love our pretty garden better than the grounds that I left."

This was her home for thirty years, till in Dec. 1851—only three years before her death—the repairs refused by Chancery made it impossible for her to risk another winter in this

" series of closets, the largest of which may be about eight feet square, which they call parlours and kitchens and pantries ; some of them minus a corner, which has been unnaturally filched for a chimney ; others deficient in half a side, which has been truncated by the shelving roof : a garden about the size of a good drawing-room, with an arbour which is a complete sentry-box of privet.

On one side a public house, on the other a villag
shop, and right opposite a cobbler's stall."

Yet she had " bright visions of a donkey-cart " ;
while " last and best of all, it was three good miles
from Reading ; that would be well enough if it
were not for the people—as rusty as old iron and as
jagged as flint stones."

But even the drastic economies of this " convenient cabin " did not set free Miss Mitford from
" literary industry." Her *Julian* was successfully
performed in 1824 ; and, in the same year, *Our
Village* appeared, to establish its author among the
famous ; extended, by 1832, to five volumes.

There can be no better description of this work
than the various comments and descriptions in her
own letters, printed below. It *is* more sentimental
than Jane Austen, or than *Cranford* ; but closely
similar in direct simplicity and truthfulness to
domestic feeling. The best of the sketches, and
many of them reach the " best," may be fairly
compared to such masterpieces ; though the
achievement is not so great, and will never be so
popular, from their lack of continued dramatic
interest, full-length characterization, and story or
plot. A collection of sketches, however perfect,
does not make a novel ; and when Miss Mitford
later attempted this higher form of fiction, she did

not—in any adequate sense—succeed. Yet *Our Village* remains unique. Nowhere else has the tranquil atmosphere of village life, with its joys and humours, its real sorrows and unexpected romances, been so lovingly and wisely portrayed. The earlier women-novelists seem, by some fortunate instinct, to have each chosen her own particular sphere for treatment, creating a corner of life for all time. Miss Mitford, of course, looked *down* on her subject, " as became a gentlewoman " ; but the sympathy and understanding are real. Since, in those days, her subjects, no less inevitably, looked *up* to her, she is not far from actual truth.

It was surely a kindly fate for one who deserved kindness, that her success came just *before* the distressing and peculiar " failing of faculty " which attacked her mother in 1825 : " She mistakes one thing for another—misjoins facts—misreports conversations—hunts for six hours together after a pincushion which she has in her pocket, or a thimble on her finger—and is totally absorbed in the smallest passing objects."

For her daughter, such a condition entailed the further worry of living beyond their means ; since any suggestion of change might " disturb, perhaps kill, her. . . . If she were herself she would rather live in a garret than run in debt ; and so would I ; merely as a question of personal comfort."

Once more Miss Mitford was driven " in the greatest hurry " to town, for the collection of money due from publishers and booksellers. Her mother lived until Jan. 1830 ; when " an attack of serious apoplexy " brought about the end : " I thought my heart would have broken, and my dear father's too."

It is not to be supposed that Dr. Mitford's grief, though no doubt perfectly genuine, would prove sufficiently prolonged to mend his ways. His daughter's anxieties were increased rather than diminished ; nor can one wonder to find her writing that " she, at forty-five, was a much older person than her own father."

She had soon to warn one of her trustees not, on any account, to " sell out her money in the funds " without direct authority : " I have no doubt of my father's integrity, but I think him likely to be imposed on." He was besides now frequently in real need of attention ; and she was compelled to devote much time to his amusement. " He could read, I think " ; but would not, and never cared for being read to except by her : " I have been obliged to read to him and play cribbage with him during more hours of each day than you could believe." When actually laid up, he would not stay " two minutes in the same posture, and not twelve minutes without getting out of bed, or up in bed, or something as bad." For herself, " The spring is broken and the watch goes down. . . . I can but last while my dear father requires me."

Dr. Mitford survived his wife twelve years, until Dec. 1842 ; when at the age of 82 he " breathed his last without a struggle or a sigh . . . almost with his own beautiful colour, the exquisite ver-milion for which he was so famous, on his sweet, serene countenance " ; but—considerably in debt.

" Everybody shall be paid," wrote Miss Mitford, " if I sell the gown off my back or pledge my little pension."

Her pension, of £100, had been applied for, and secured, in 1837. Her case had been taken up by those to whom she somewhat quaintly expresses her thanks :

" Is not this very honourable to the kind feelings of our aristocracy ? I always knew that I had, as a writer, a strong hold in that quarter ; that they turned with disgust from the trash called fashion-able novels to the common life of Miss Austen, the Irish Tales of Miss Edgeworth, and my humble village stories ; but I did not suspect the strong personal interest which these stories have excited, and I am immensely grateful for it."

The sum, indeed, was small ; and on her father's death some of " the aristocracy," Mrs. Browning's friend Kenyon, Thomas Moore, and Sergeant Talfourd, joined with other friends in an *Appeal*

to the Public for the payment of debts left by the
doctor : " That which would fall with a crushing
weight upon one solitary and almost destitute
woman, will be but little felt when divided among
the affluent and the many." The response was
generous enough for the occasion.

Despite the strain, Miss Mitford never neglected
her work or her friends, during this period or in
the thirteen years left to her ; and it would be
untrue to deny that she was able to gain much
pleasure from both. Though in her black moods
she declared that " Nothing seems to me so melan-
choly as the lives of authors," and that " all literary
people die overwrought—it is the destiny of the
class," she was enthusiastic in her friendship, for
instance, with Mrs. Browning, delighted with young
Ruskin, and other congenial spirits : often starting
correspondence with persons on either side of the
Atlantic whom she had never met. She had long
ago reversed the drastic sentence of 1818—" with
one exception I never saw an American gentleman
in my life. They are a second-hand, pawnbroker's
shop kind of nation—a nation without literature,
without art, and totally unconscious of the beautiful
nature by which they are surrounded."

She enjoyed the sweets of popularity, and a
pilgrimage to " Three Miles Cross " had become
something of an institution. If " within one week

a young friend had asked her to edit her poems, another to write up and present her Tragedy, a third person (whom she had never seen) to read an MS. novel " ; on the other hand, " very few ever went away disappointed from the narrow, comfortless, presence-chamber of the grey-haired lady, who beamed upon her guests from ' that wonderful wall of a forehead,' and welcomed them so cordially with a most admirable voice."

She could now speak with astonishment of a three-halfpenny periodical like *Chambers's Edinburgh Journal* " engaging so high-priced a writer as herself " ; she produced a tragedy and an opera ; gardeners were " constantly calling plants after her " ; " four of the crack artists of the exhibition " were painting in the little household, including Landseer, her favourite ; her *Country Stories* were to be reissued " for a shilling, or perhaps ninepence — that being the price of Miss Austen's novels " ; and her *Recollections* were in great demand.

Her industry, indeed, never flagged ; and it *was* wonderful, as she says, that " in a twelvemonth " she should " have written *Otto, Country Stories, The Tableaux*, and a story (longer than a Tableaux) *lost* in the road to Edinburgh, or at Edinburgh—at any rate lost ; a loss, first and last, of above seventy pounds." On one occasion, when a " book was

finished somehow," she found herself, " at the last,
incapable of correcting the proofs, literally fainting
on the ground."

There was now " a very pathetic expression about
her mouth and in her large, slowly moving, sad,
grey eyes, though they lighted up every now and
then with a glancing gleam of the drollest humour."

Her absolute incapacity for dressing suitably, or
even tidily, must have added considerably to the
pathetic appearance of the lonely old lady ; perhaps
the more from her being quite unconscious of the
quaint figure she so often presented.

It was during the last ten years of her life, however, that she first met the intrepid climber and
chamois hunter, Charles Boner, who translated
Hans Andersen ; and whose *Memoirs* contain two
hundred pages of her letters.   The habit of reading
and criticizing books is here revealed with no less
energy than at any period of her life ; equally
potent with the gift for friendship.

Fate, or some unexplained freakish spirit of
adventure, involved her, during one summer,
1841, in a serious fright from a runaway horse ;
being " dragged over the rafters in an unfloored
room across the joists, a depth of four feet and a
half—a terrible jar upon the spine " ; and setting
" the frill of her nightcap " on fire, when " everybody was in bed and asleep," so that she had to

" fling herself upon the ground and extinguish it
with the hearthrug."

One more move came in 1850, to a charming
cottage at Swallowfield; and after a period of
dependence upon being wheeled about in a bath-
chair, she died " so peacefully that she hardly knew
which moment was her last," in her sixty-eighth
year, on Jan. 10, 1855.

" It was a great, warm, outflowing heart," wrote
Mrs. Browning, " and the head was worthy of the
heart. . . . I agree with you that she was stronger
and wider in her conversation than in her books.
Oh ! I have said so a hundred times. The heart
of human sympathy seemed to bring out her
powerful vitality, rustling all over with laces and
flowers."

R. BRIMLEY JOHNSON.

LETTERS

From Mary Russell Mitford, in her eleventh year, to her Father

HANS PLACE, *Sept.* 15, 1799.

MY DEAR PAPA,

I sit down in order to return you thanks for the parcels I received. My uncle called on me twice while he stayed in London, but he went away in five minutes both times. He said that he only went to fetch my aunt, and would certainly take me out when he returned. I hope that I may be wrong in my opinion of my aunt ; but I again repeat, I think she has the most hypocritical drawl that I ever heard. Pray, my dearest papa, come soon to see me. I am quite miserable without you, and have a thousand things to say to you. I suppose that you will pass almost all your time at Odiam this season, as it is a very good country for sporting ; and that family is so agreeable, that it would be very pleasant for mamma to stay there with you.

Remember me to all the family, particularly to grandpapa and William.

Feb. 23, 1801.

I really think that my dearly-beloved mother had better have the jackasses than the cart-horses. The former will at least have the recommendation of singularity, which the other has not ; as I am convinced that more than half the smart carriages in the neighbourhood of Reading are drawn by the horses which work in the team.

March 23, 1802.

I hope dear old Tod [her father] will take care of his sweet head ! His poor Mam Bonette is not able to fly, or she certainly would come to Reading to nurse him, and she is the only one that nurses him well. But dear Mumper [her mother] must not be jealous, as she knows his Mam was always his head nurse—I hope you will be obliged to take down your house at the farm. It will be much better to have it all new together.

Dec. 16, 1802.

I have just received your letters, and thank you again and again for them. I cannot find terms to express my gratitude and my affection to my darling parents, and therefore must pass them over in silence. I shall most certainly be at liberty by two o'clock ; but I hope you know me well enough to be assured that it is the pleasure of embracing my sweet mother which makes me anxious to come, and not of going to the ball, to which I certainly shall not go. I have been invited to go to the Harness's to-day, but refused, and promised that, if you were disengaged, we would go to dinner there on Friday. So you see I am already getting a great lady, making, accepting, or refusing engagements according to my fancy.

To Mrs. Mitford, Bertram House

LITTLE HARLE TOWER, *Oct.* 3, 1806.
Friday morning.

I received yesterday, my dearest darling, your very long letter, and am charmed to find you amuse yourself so well during our absence. We took a long walk on Wednesday morning, and got very wet ; and the scenery, though extremely beautiful, by no means compensated me for all the mud I was forced to wade through. Lady Charles minds it no more than a duck ; but I have begged to be excused from such excursions for the future. As I was changing my wet clothes, Colonel and Mrs. Beaumont called on their way to Kirk Harle to apologize for not spending the next day here, as they are obliged unexpectedly to go into Yorkshire immediately. Of course then I did not see them ; but we met at dinner at Sir William Lorraine's ; and Mrs. B. was so polite as to express great regret that, as she was going from home, she could not see us at her house, but hoped, when next we came to Northumberland, we should come to see them at Hexham Abbey. She is a very sweet woman. We had a very pleasant party—not at all formal— Sir W. and Lady Lorraine, Mr. and Mrs. Lorraine (his eldest son and his wife, who live with Sir W.), Mr. John Lorraine, the Beaumonts, and ourselves.

Mrs. B. told Lady Charles that they received last year a hundred thousand pounds from their lead mines in Yorkshire ; and they never make less than eighty thousand, independently of immense incomes from their other estates. Mrs. B. was dressed in a lavender-coloured satin, with Mechlin lace, long sleeves, and a most beautiful Mechlin veil. The necklace she wore was purchased by her eldest son, a boy of eleven, who sent it from the jeweller's without asking the price. It is of most beautiful amethysts ; the three middle stones are an inch and a half long and an inch wide ; the price was nine hundred guineas. Mrs. B. wished to return it ; but the Colonel not only confirmed the purchase, but gave his son some thousands to complete the set of amethysts by a bandeau and tiara, a cestus for the waist, armlets, bracelets, brooches, sleeve-clasps, and shoe-knots. All these she wore, and I must confess, for a small dinner-party appeared rather too gaily decorated, particularly as Lady Lorraine's dress was quite in the contrary extreme. I never saw so strong a contrast. Her ladyship is a small, delicate woman, and Mrs. B. large and strong ; and she wore a plain cambric gown and a small chip hat, without any sort of ornament either on her head or neck. Colonel Beaumont is generally supposed to be extremely weak ; and I had heard so much of him, that I expected to see at least as silly a man as Matthew Robinson ; but I sat next him at dinner, and he conducted himself with infinite propriety

and great attention and politeness ; yet, when away
from Mrs. Beaumont, he is (they say) quite foolish,
and owes everything to her influence with him.
They live in immense style at the Abbey ; thirty
or forty persons frequently dine there ; no servants
but their own admitted ; and there is constantly
a footman behind every chair. I hope I have not
tired you with this long account ; but they are the
principal people in the neighbourhood, and I know
my own darling is always pleased to know among
whom her Twart [1] is thrown.

Yesterday morning was extremely fine, and Lady
Charles ordered her landaulet at twelve, and took
papa and me to call at Wallington, the very beautiful
seat of Sir John Trevelyan, who has given it up to
his eldest son.   Mr. T. was at home, and Lady C.,
in order to show me the house, went in and saw him.
It is indeed extremely magnificent, and has been
fitted up this summer in all the splendour of
Egyptian decoration. There are three very large
drawing-rooms, a fine dining-room, study, &c.
We then drove to Capheaton (Sir John Swinburne's).
The family were out, but we admired the park, and
drove home by the lake, which covers forty or fifty
acres, and is beautifully diversified with islands
bordered by fine woods.   The ride altogether was
through as picturesque a country as I ever saw ;
and I was greatly disappointed that to-day being
wet prevented our going to Belsay Castle, the
seat of Sir Charles Monck. The Squire of the

---

[1] Another of her own pet names.

Castle [1] arrived here yesterday.   He and Lord C. are
shooting, and papa and his dear godson—the finest
boy you ever saw—are coursing.   I told you I was
not enamoured of Mr. M., and I will now describe
him to you.   In person he something resembles Mr.
P—— ; but he is an oddity from affectation ; and,
I often think, no young man affects singularity
when he can distinguish himself by anything better.
He affects to despise women, yet treats them
with great respect ; and he makes the most extraordinary assertions to provoke an argument,
from which he generally escapes by some whimsical
phrase.

   To-morrow I go to Morpeth ; on Monday Miss
Mitford and I go to Kirkley, and on Wednesday
we both come here, to go to Alnwick on Thursday.
On Saturday we return to Morpeth for a few days,
but soon come back here, to go to Lord Grey's and
Admiral Roddam's.   Lady Charles would not part
with me at all if she were not afraid of offending her
father and mother ; and, as it is, I shall be a week
at Little Harle for a day at Morpeth.   You perceive,
my dear, sweet darling, that the plan of going to
Alnwick is changed ; we now go next Thursday,
in order to avoid sleeping there, which we must
have done if we had gone there at the same time
as to Lord Grey's ; and it will, I think, be much
pleasanter.   When I return we are to have a fishing
party on Sir John Swinburne's lake.

   [1] Mitford of Mitford Castle.

To Mrs. Mitford, Bertram House

LITTLE HARLE TOWER, *Nov.* 2, 1806.
Sunday morning.

The promising appearance of yesterday morning, my dearest mamma, tempted us to set forward on our expedition to Hexham. On our arrival we drove immediately to the Abbey, where Colonel Beaumont had arrived only the night before. Mrs. Beaumont remains in Yorkshire. The Colonel was delighted to see us, and pressed us much to stay dinner. This we, of course, refused, as it was rather too much to travel twenty miles after a six o'clock dinner. We, however, accepted his offer of seeing the beautiful church which joins his house ; and Lady Charles took me to see the Abbey itself. Upon repairing and beautifying this house, in which they only spend about a month in the year, the poor Colonel has lately expended upwards of twelve thousand pounds. It was a fine specimen of the Saxon Gothic architecture ; but he has built upon the same foundation, retained all the inconveniences of the ancient style, and lost all its grandeur. It has on the outside an appearance of a manufactory, and the inside conveys the exact idea of an inn. I should have thought it absolutely impossible to construct so bad a house with so many rooms. There is but one good one, which is the ball-room, and this is made the passage to the bedchambers. Yet this is the occasional residence of a man with an income of a hundred and ten thousand pounds ;

the residence where he receives the visits of all his constituents in this large and opulent county ; and where he lives in the most princely magnificence. In order to render the bad taste of this abominable modern house still more conspicuous, it is contrasted with the singular beauty of the adjoining cathedral, whose gloomy magnificence and fine pointed arches delighted me extremely. The Colonel is the patron, I may almost say the proprietor, of this fine church (for he is what they call a lay bishop, and still receives the tributary pence from the communicants) ; yet that part of the edifice where the pews are placed is in a most shocking state. The bottom of one of the pews, situated exactly under his own, is covered with straw like a London hackney coach ; and even his own pew seems quietly resigned to the moths and other depredators. Everything, in short, seemed to testify it was a place he seldom visited.

We dined at a very wretched inn, for I must confess, in spite of the prepossession I felt in favour of my dear Ittey's native town, that Hexham is a shocking gloomy place. After dinner I had the pleasure of visiting the house where my darling was born. It has been an extremely good one, and still retains a very respectable appearance ; but it is now divided, and on one side of the street door, which still remains, is a collar maker's shop, and on the other a milliner's. We entered the latter and purchased three pair of Hexham gloves, one for papa, one for my dearest mamma, and one for

Ammy. I thought that, both as a memorial of the town and of the house, you would like that better than any other trifle I could procure. Our return was very tedious and disagreeable ; but I was gratified on my arrival by finding a letter from papa, directed to Morpeth, in which he promises to be there as to-day. I cannot think, my darling, why you did not send him off on Wednesday, for the eating and drinking, and bawling at the election will do him more harm than twenty journeys. Gog,[1] he says, is very ill. God forgive me, but I do not pity him. He deserves some punishment for endeavouring to play such a trick upon papa and me. To-morrow is the Morpeth election ; so papa will have his favourite passion gratified by being present at that also. Lord and Lady Charles will take me in with them to-morrow. I should quit this house with great regret did I not hope to be on my return to my beloved mamma by the latter end of the week.

To Dr. Mitford, Richardson's Hotel

BERTRAM HOUSE, *April* 10, 1807.

A thousand thanks, my beloved, for your very kind and entertaining letter. We rejoiced to find you had relinquished all thoughts of mobbing it to the House, which would have been a most fatiguing and tiresome exertion ; and, since the *great* speakers

[1] A nickname among the Mitfords for their friend Mr. Shaw Lefevre.

are gone, it would most likely have met with an
inadequate reward. What Grattan may be when
speaking upon so interesting a subject as places and
pensions, I know not ; but when he was brought in
last Parliament to display his powers upon the
Catholic question (which is, I admit, to party men
a subject of very inferior importance), the House
was extremely disappointed. If I remember rightly,
he was characterized as a " little, awkward, fidgety,
petulant speaker " ; and the really great man who
then led the Opposition easily dispensed with his
assistance. Pray, whom do you include in the
Prince's party ? but many would-be placemen will,
I dare say, be sufficiently ready to court the rising
sun.   It used to be by no means a numerous one ;
mamma insists that Charles Fox used to belong to
it. This I dispute *in toto* ; but I shall be much
obliged to you to settle our debate.   It is true that
the Prince inclined much more to Fox than Pitt,
and his people generally voted with the former ;
but Mr. Fox never was in his secrets, and he would
have disclaimed with indignation the crooked policy
of the heir apparent.

You wish to know what I thought of the Lefevres'
visit ; and I assure you, my dear darling, that I
think just the same of them now as I did before.
They were (excepting in one instance, which is too
long to detail in a letter) tolerably civil ; and
Mr. Lefevre sported some intolerably bad puns,
which were, I suppose, intended for our entertain-
ment ; but they did not discompose my gravity.

In short, I believe that he has no inclination to meet you, and was glad to find you were in town.   Little minds always wish to avoid those to whom they are under obligations ; and his present " trimming " in politics must conspire to render him still more desirous not to meet you, till he has found which party is *strongest*. That will, I am of opinion, decide which he will espouse.

Now for domestic news.   Our family has been increased this morning by the birth of a calf.   I saw it conducted home in triumph in a wheel-barrow, and followed by its fond mamma (little Mary), and the other cows.   Heaven bless you, my beloved !   We long for your return, and are ever most fondly

MARY RUSSELL MITFORD.
MARY MITFORD.

To Dr. Mitford, Richardson's Hotel

BERTRAM HOUSE, *April* 15, 1807.

The debate in the House of Lords is, as you observe, my beloved darling, extremely interesting. I perfectly agree with you as to the great merit of Lord Erskine's very eloquent speech.   It does him the greatest credit ; and, as he was against the Catholic question, his opinions will have more weight with the country than those of any other of the ex-ministers.   I always thought Lord Sidmouth a very bad speaker.   His sun is set, never, I hope,

to rise again !   Mr. S Lefevre's speech is worthy
of attention, as being to the full as incomprehensible
as that of his worthy colleague upon a late occasion.
In fact, I would defy the most expert solver of
enigmas to resolve the question of which side he
meant to support.   Do you remember the definition of " modern candour " in Mr. Canning's *New
Morality* ?   The member for Reading seems to
have laid claim to this virtue in its highest perfection.
According to him :

> Black 's not so black, nor white so very white.

In short, the more I know of this gentleman the
more I am convinced that, under a roughness of
manner, he conceals a very extraordinary pliancy
of principles and a very accommodating conscience.
He holds in contempt the old-fashioned manly
virtues of firmness and consistency, and is truly
" a vane changed by every wind."   If he votes with
the Opposition to-day, it will only be because he
thinks them likely to be again in power ; and it will,
I really think, increase my contempt for him, if
he does not do so.

There is an excellent letter in the *Chronicle*
to-day, purporting to come from the " chef de
cuisine " at the Foreign Office.   According to that,
neither Mr. Canning nor Mr. Hammond speak
French.   This is, I think, hardly possible.

To Sir William Elford, Bart., Bickham, Plymouth

BERTRAM HOUSE, *Sept.* 20, 1810.

If I had the presumption to differ from you on the merits of Miss Holford's poem, my dear sir, I completely agree in the justice and discrimination of your critique on *The Lady of the Lake*. The singular want of invention in the similarity of the two surprises had quite escaped me, though I have read the whole poem aloud three several times ; so careless a reader am I ! But I have since re-collected a still more extraordinary circumstance. The *dénouement* of *Marmion* and that of *The Lay of the Last Minstrel* both turn on the same discovery. This repetition is wonderful in a man of so much genius, and the more so as the incident is in itself so stale, so like the foolish trick of a pantomime, that to have used it once was once too often.

I quite agree with you in your admiration of Miss Edgeworth. She and Miss Baillie and Mrs. Opie are three such women as have seldom adorned one age and one country. Of the three, I think I had rather (if such a metamorphosis were possible) resemble Miss Baillie. Yet Mrs. Opie is certainly not the least accomplished of the trio, and Miss Edgeworth has done more good both to the higher and lower world than any writer since the days of Addison. She shoots at " folly as it flies " with the strong bolt of ridicule, and seldom misses her aim. Perhaps you will think that I betray a strange want

of taste when I confess that, much as I admire the
polished satire and nice discrimination of character
in the *Tales of Fashionable Life*, I prefer the homely
pathos and plain morality of her *Popular Tales* to
any part of her last publication. The story of
"Rosanna" is particularly delightful to me; and that
of "To-morrow" made so deep an impression on my
mind, that, if it were possible for any earthly power
to reform a procrastinator, I really think that tale
would have cured me of my evil habits.   I actually
rose two mornings a full hour before my usual time
after reading it—pray, my dear sir, do not ask me
what that hour is.   The victims of *ennui* are found
all over England, from the peer to the farmer, if
the latter is unfortunately rich enough to exempt
him from personal labour and pecuniary anxiety.
The physicians have already recognized it as a
disease ; and I expect we shall soon see " died of
ennui " placed in the bills of mortality.

A poor little nabob who lives in Reading lately
consulted an eminent medical practitioner on a
dizziness which he had contracted by riding in a
barouche from Brighton to Rottingdean, on an
excursion of pleasure undertaken for the express
purpose of driving away " the foul fiend."   The
doctor's prescription was very rational and very
uncommon.   " You had much to do in India,
Mr. W—— ? "   " Oh, yes.   I fagged eight hours
a day."   " Well, sir, you must either resume your
post there, or get employment here, or turn hypo-
chondriac."   I have not yet heard his determina-

tion ; but, poor man, he had just made a fortune,
and come home to enjoy it. He is married, too,
unluckily ; so that there are no hopes of his reliev-
ing the tedium of domestic peacefulness by a little
female ratiocination.   A scolding wife is an infallible
recipe.   The manœuvrers, thank Heaven ! are not
quite so numerous ; but we have one in our
neighbourhood who bears so strong a resemblance
to Mrs. Beaumont,[1] that, as the lady is originally
from Ireland, half the families in the county suspected that Miss Edgeworth had drawn not from
the species but the individual, and that her picture
would never have had so much truth and nature
had she not both sketched and coloured it from our
exquisite " neighbour."   She has two most charming daughters, who, though dragged to town every
spring ; to some watering-place every autumn ;
and to all the parties, plays, concerts, and balls
within twenty miles of their home here, during the
rest of the year : still remain in " single blessedness," to the indescribable mortification of their
mamma, and to the great discredit of her inimitable
talents for plots, schemes, and puffing, match
making, and match-breaking.   As she is really a
very sensible woman, I wonder she does not begin
to suspect that she has taken a wrong method to get
these sweet girls well married.   Nothing could
account for the circumstance of two such very
lovely young women having reached the age of
twenty without attracting one serious admirer but

[1] The heroine of Miss Edgeworth's *Manœuvring*.

the circumstance of their being the daughters of a manœuvrer.

My dear papa, I am afraid, led you to expect that I had made a greater progress in *Christina* than I have really done.   It is true that in a fortnight I wrote a thousand lines (such as they are), which, considering that we keep early hours, and that either from habit or caprice I can never write till candle-light, is really very tolerable work.   But I am sorry to say, my dear sir, that I have scarcely written a hundred lines since, having been engaged in our annual dissipation of balls and concerts, races and oratorios.   Oh, the dear delights of a music meeting! Sitting next to your grocer's wife with a silver cap on her head and a crescent of Dovey's diamonds stuck in the front of it!   Jammed in between brewers and bakers, and tailors and corndealers ; or dancing among their spruce sons and over-dressed daughters, who either dislocate your arms in turning you round, or tread your toes off in threading the intricacies of right-hand and left !   It is well for you that my waning paper saves you from a dissertation on the follies of a country town, and brings this tiresome letter to an end.   A tiresome letter has been compared to a tedious visit ; but there is this happy difference, that the paper torment may be cut short by throwing it into the fire or out of the window, whilst you could not so well get rid of the writer in that way, both on account of her being rather a weighty concern, and of your well-known politeness.

Adieu, my dear sir !   Papa and mamma beg me
to present their best respects ; and I am ever, with
every sentiment of esteem,

Very sincerely yours,

MARY RUSSELL MITFORD.

To Dr. Mitford, New Slaughter's Coffee House

August 8, 1811.

Mamma says the great art of letter-writing is to
construct an epistle without one possible subject.
And truly, if such be the fact, no two people have
a better opportunity of improving in this way than
those who have the honour of sending you a sheet
full of nothings.   Indeed, my dearest love, upon a
careful revision of our letters, I do not suppose that
upon an average they would be found to contain
one piece of intelligence a week ; unless, indeed,
you may call it news to hear that our *ci-devant*
dairymaid Harriet, who has now the honour of
assisting in Mrs. Curtis's seminary for young ladies,
is reported to have consented, at the request of her
admirer, William, to leave her place at Michaelmas
in order to share his fate and Mrs. Adams's cottage.
God help them, poor fools ; what will become of
them !   Two such dawdles never existed.

Marmion is more beautiful than ever.   He will
certainly win the cup at Ilsley this year.   I hope
you mean to run him, my pet.   He has an hereditary claim to it.

Fanny Rowden cannot mean to assert that all who

have breathed the air of 22 Hans Place must be
female Solomons ! If she does, Heaven help her !
Don Quixote, when he took the fair nymph of the
inn for the daughter of the Governor of the Castle,
did not make a greater mistake. I am very anxious
to see the *Triumphs of Religion*. Miss Cope has
reaped a golden harvest ; but I am much mistaken
if *Suicide* be equally successful. Those sort of
begging experiments never answer above once.

Mammy and all the pets desire their love. · They
are all well.

> Ever and ever,
> Most fondly and faithfully your own,
> MARY RUSSELL MITFORD.

To Sir William Elford, Bickham, Plymouth

BERTRAM HOUSE, *August* 18, 1811.

I was from former experience, my dear sir,
almost certain that your silence was accidental,
though the precise cause I could not determine.

I must caution you against expecting the poem
to be even so good as the specimen. It will be
nothing less than brilliant. That poor little sylph-
like thing is destined to go through almost every
misfortune that can be named. Pandora's box is
opened upon her ; and to illustrate the true
feminine courage of patient endurance in an interesting and pathetic tale, is the whole object of my
poem. This is strongly contrasted with the joyous
brilliancy of her station and person. The truth is,

that I am fond of that species of moral antithesis
(if I may use the expression) which results from
contrast of situation and of feeling and of external
nature, with the beings who inhabit it. You will
find a great deal of this in *Blanch* ; but, woe is me !
Blanch is to consist of five thousand lines, and only
eleven hundred are yet written !

Have you read *Self-Control* ? You do read
novels sometimes ; so I may venture to ask the
question without offending against the dignity of
your sex.   I wrote lately to a fair cousin of mine in
Scotland, and asked her the same question.   She
could not give her own sentiments, but she wrote
me a most curious account of a dispute, which
Miss Wilson's much-talked-of book had occasioned
between two gentlemen, one of whom said it ought
to be burnt by the common hangman, and the other
that it ought to be written in letters of gold.   What
a high opinion would this have given me of the
work, if I had not read it ! Having read it, my
sentiments accord with neither.   I would only send
it to the pastrycook and the trunkmaker—am I not
merciful ?   My fair correspondent tells me that the
good folks in Edinburgh prefer *Don Roderick* to any
of Walter Scott's former productions.   I think it is
not very presumptuous to prophesy that this extraordinary preference will not extend southward.
There never was a greater falling-off.   It is not
only more careless and incorrect than his former
poems (and they, Heaven knows ! were careless
enough), but it wants the glow, the spirit, the power

over the imagination and the heart, which, with all his faults, Mr. Scott certainly possesses in an eminent degree. Even the metre is defective in sweetness, and sometimes in dignity.

Have you seen Miss Seward's Letters ? The names of her correspondents are tempting, but, alas ! though addressed to all the eminent literati of the last half-century, all the epistles bear the signature of Anna Seward. To tell you the truth, I was always a little shocked at the sort of reputation she bore in poetry. Sometimes affected, sometimes *fade*, sometimes pedantic, and sometimes tinselly, none of her works were ever simple, graceful, or natural ; and I never heard her praised but I fancied the commendation would end in, " It is very well —for a woman ! " What I have seen of her letters confirms me in this idea. They are affected, sentimental, and lackadaisical to the highest degree ; and her taste is even worse than her execution. She, Anna Seward, sees nothing to admire in Cowper's letters !—in letters (the playful ones, of course, I mean) which would have immortalized him, had *The Task* never been written, and which (much as I admire the playful wit of the two illustrious namesakes, Lady M. W. and Mrs. Montagu) are, in my opinion, the only perfect specimens of epistolary composition in the English language. They are, in short, what the letters of Madame de Sévigné are in French. You must know, my dear sir, that I have a theory respecting letter-writing, though, like most theorists, my practice differs most unhappily from my principles. " *Rien n'est beau que le vrai ; le vrai seul est aimable*," is my motto ; and translating " *le vrai*," rather according to the spirit than the letter, by " the natural," I believe that you will agree with me. According to my theory, letters should assimilate to the higher style of conversation, without the snip-snap of fashionable dialogue, and with more of the simple transcripts of natural feeling than the usage of good society would authorize. Playfulness is preferable to wit, and grace infinitely more desirable than precision. A little egotism, too, must be admitted ; without it, a letter would stiffen into a treatise, and a billet assume " the form and pressure " of an essay.

I have often thought a fictitious correspondence (not a novel, observe) between two ladies or gentlemen, consisting of a little character, a little description, a little narrative, a little criticism, a very little sentiment and a great deal of playfulness, would be a very pleasing and attractive work : " A very good article, sir " (to use the booksellers' language) ; " one that would go off rapidly—pretty light summer reading for the watering-places and the circulating libraries." If I had the slightest idea that I could induce you to undertake such a work by coaxing, by teasing, or by scolding (and in naming these I have almost exhausted the whole female artillery), you should have no quarter from me till you had promised or produced it. In the meanwhile it is time that I should release you from this farrago

of nonsense and criticism, and I will at least conclude with that which must always be " *le vrai*,"
by assuring my own kind friend with how much
sincerity I am ever

His obliged and affectionate
Mary Russell Mitford.

To Sir William Elford, Bickham, Plymouth

Bertram House, *Dec.* 15, 1811.

Your most kind letter followed me to London,
where I have been staying for the last ten days. I
went thither for a purpose which, I think, was
extremely soberminded and praiseworthy ; albeit
I never mentioned it to any one that did not laugh
in my face. I went thither to improve in my voca-
tion (just as country milliners and mantua-makers
go to *finish* and learn fashions) by hearing divers
lectures—on Milton and Shakespeare, and criticism
and poetry, and poets and critics, and whipping
little boys, and love and philosophy, and every
subject that ever entered the head of man—from
my good friend Mr. Coleridge. And here I am
returned quite Coleridgified ; much in the same
way, I suppose, as Boswell was after a visit to
Johnson ; sprinkling, but not mixing, his brilliancy
with my dulness, " like sprigs of embroidery on a
ground of linsey-woolsey."

What a simpleton I am to tell you all this ! I
shall not say a pretty thing to you for these six

months, but you will give the credit of it to my
dearly-beloved lecturer. I wish you had heard
him. You would certainly have been enchanted ;
for, though his lectures are desultory in the highest
degree, and though his pronunciation is an odd
mixture of all that is bad in the two worst dialects
of England, the Somersetshire and the Westmoreland, with an addition, which I believe to be
exclusively his own, namely giving to the *a* long
as in " wave " and " bane," a sound exactly resembling that which children make in imitating
the bleating of a sheep, " ba-a-a " ; yet in spite of
all these defects, he has so much of the electric
power of genius—that power which fixes the
attention by rousing at once the fancy and the
heart — that the ear has scarcely the wish to
condemn that which so strongly delights the
intellect.

I must tell you a misadventure which happened
to me at one of these lectures. I had set my heart
on taking my friend Mrs. Rowden with me. Now,
she is about as difficult to draw as a road waggon
(not personally, but mentally, I mean), and had no
fancy for the expedition ; but as she had to do with
one quite as obstinate, and a thousand times more
enthusiastic than herself, I carried my point, and
had the satisfaction of seating her close by my side
in the lecture-room. It was very full. The orator
was more than usually brilliant ; and I had just
got Mrs. R. to confess that " he really was tolerable " (a wonderful confession, considering she

was *a lady*, and determined to dislike him), when to my utter dismay he began a period as follows : " There are certain poems—or things called poems —which have obtained considerable fame—or that which is called fame—in the world ; I mean the Pleasures of Tea-drinking, and the Pleasures of Wine-drinking, and the Pleasures of Love, and the Pleasures of Nonsense, and the Pleasures of Hope." There, thank God, the list ended, for his censure was only aimed at Campbell, whom he proceeded to abuse.   But think what I felt while he was going on with his " Pleasures," and I expected the " Pleasures of Friendship " to come out every moment.   Mr. Rogers was just by, so that Mrs. Rowden had the comfort of company in her sensations, whatever they might be ; but they had both the wit to keep them to themselves.

I dare say, my dear Sir William, that you know more of town news at Bickham than I did in London, though I heard plenty of it ; but I am sadly troubled with " the malady of not marking."   I can only tell you that everybody goes to see some beautiful specimens of French engraving, especially some portraits of the Emperor, of which you may possess yourself at the moderate price of a hundred guineas each ; that one is wearied to death with the dis-putes[1] respecting Dr. Bell and Mr. Lancaster ; and that it is said to be as difficult to get a box to see Mrs. Siddons, as it was to see the young Roscius of notorious memory.   However, I contrived to

[1] On Education.

obtain a place, and saw her ; and (for the first time in my life) without pleasure, in *Pizarro*. I had never before seen that disgrace to Kotzebue, to Sheridan, to the stage, and to the audience ; and I really think the horses of last year, and the elephants of this, are rational amusements compared to the penance of hearing such rhodomontade from human organs.

Poor Marmion is much obliged to you for your good wishes, and so is his mistress ; but, alas ! they are unavailing. You must know, my dear sir, that papa contrived to lame him among the nasty Hampshire flints just the week before the Ilsley meeting, and he has just played the same prank with poor Maria. Is not he a very naughty man ? Believe me to be always

Most sincerely and affectionately yours,

MARY RUSSELL MITFORD.

If I had but two inches of paper, then would I tell you of a marriage about to take place in our family ; but, alas ! I have no frank, and what woman was ever brief in announcing a wedding ? I must, however, squeeze in, that my dear cousin, Charlotte Murray (the prettiest girl in Scotland— if you wish to see her picture look at Scott's *Lady of the Lake*) is going to be married to a General Oswald (do you know him ?), and that her uncle, the Duke of Athole, gives five hundred pounds for her wedding-clothes.

To Sir William Elford, Bickham, Plymouth

BERTRAM HOUSE, *Jan.* 5, 1812

MY DEAR SIR WILLIAM,

Have you read *The Countess and Gertrude*, a philosophical novel of much note ? I have no patience with it ; because, in the first place, it abuses spoilt children, and you and I know that spoilt children are sometimes very innocent little simpletons ; in the second, it advises a sort of rigorous discipline during youth, in order to prepare for the misfortunes of age. By-the-way, this is just such an argument as it would have been, before inoculation was practised, to have advised a man to live all his life on panada and water-gruel, for fear he should have the small-pox in an unprepared state ; and it would entirely annihilate all the happiness of the only truly happy part of our existence. And is not the sunny felicity of child-hood in itself unconscious virtue ? Is it not con-nected with every sweet, and generous, and unselfish feeling ? And is it not the parent of that general love, that Scriptural charity, without which there is in this life neither happiness nor virtue ?

Did I not puzzle you a little in my last by talking of Mr. Coleridge lecturing upon whipping ? The fact is, that he actually began one of his orations by a very eloquent but rather laughable panegyric on the practice of flogging schoolboys, in preference to Mr. Lancaster's method of shaming children by various devices. I am a steady Lancasterian—I always loved " the red, red rose " ; and yet it brought forcibly to my recollection a most laughable failure of a punishment of this sort, in which I was a party concerned.

You must know, my dear Sir William (to tell a story of the good old gossiping style), that the mansion where I had the honour to be initiated into the mysteries of grammars, globes, and dictionaries was, like most other mansions of the same sort, kept by a governess and governed by her teachers. Of these, the French *gouvernante* (called in school-girl jargon " madame ") was always *la dame dominante* ; and when I first left home, I found in that situation a lovely, heartbroken young woman, the daughter of an *émigré* of distinction, worn down by her parents' distresses, and her own inability to alleviate them, and totally unable to contend with the thoughtless levity of twenty gay and unmanage-able children. The English assistant was exactly of that character which had rather do a thing than undertake the trouble of seeing that another did it ; just the sort of woman who, had she been in the far more enviable post of a nursery-maid, would have nursed a child into the rickets sooner than teach it to walk. She took care to put by everything after us, or to order the servants to do so ; all appeared well and orderly in the sight of the governess ; and, while the sweet Mlle La Roche stayed, all was quiet. She was fortunate enough in the short Peace of Amiens to get to France with her father and mother,

and recover part of her paternal possessions ; whilst
with her unhappy pupils, the dominion of King
Log was succeeded by that of King Stork. The
" madame " that came was a fine majestic-looking
old woman of sixty, but with all the activity of
sixteen, and the fidgety neatness of a Dutch woman.
Four days passed on in distant murmurs at our
untidy habits, and threats of a terrible example to
be made of those who left things " *traînantes par la
chambre.*" A few exercise books found out of place
were thrown into the fire, and a few skipping-ropes
(one of which had nearly broken " madame's "
neck by her falling over it in the dark) thrown out
of the window. But all this was but the gathering
of the wind before a storm. It was dancing day.
We were all dressed and assembled in the room,
when " madame," to our unspeakable consterna-
tion, began a thorough rummage all over the house
and called us to follow her. Oh ! the hats, the
tippets, the shoes, the gloves, the books, the music,
the playthings and the workthings, that this unlucky
search discovered thrown into holes, and corners,
and everywhere but where they ought to have been !
Well, my dear sir, all this immense quantity of litter
was to be fastened to the person and the dress of the
unfortunate little urchin to whom it belonged.
The task of apportioning it was, indeed, much such
an one as a malevolent fairy in one of Madame
D'Aunois' Fairy Tales assigned to a captive princess
when she brought her the mixed plumages belonging
to several different birds, and ordered her to assign

every single feather to its proper proprietor. But,
alas ! poor " madame " did not know the plumage
of her little birds, and she had no good genius to
assist her in the task ; for " *ce n'est pas à moi* " was
all she could get from the little delinquents, and
many were the hats that no one would claim, and
the gloves that no one would own, and the slippers
which, like the famous glass one, would fit nobody.
Plenty, however, remained, which could not be
denied, to form a style of decoration more novel
than elegant. Dictionaries suspended from the
neck *en médaillon*, shawls tied round the waist *en
ceinture*, the loose pieces of music pinned to the
frock *en queue*, formed but a small part of this
adornment. There were few that had not two or
three of these elegant appendages, and many had
five or six. I escaped the best, from a cause that
is pretty general in this world—because, in short,
my sins were of the greatest magnitude. One of
the maids took care of my clothes, and I took care
not to own my garden habiliments. Work I never
touched, so I could not leave that about ; and as to
my music-books, they might have stayed untouched
in their places from Midsummer to Christmas had
I not been obliged, *malgré moi*, to make use of them.
Nothing of this, therefore, was found against me ;
but in the very middle of the dancing room, just
opposite to a large French window, was a table with
an old portfolio almost as big as myself, a glass of
dirty water, and a plate on which I had been mixing
colours. None of these seemed portable. To be

sure, if " madame " had been well read in *Don Quixote* she might have encased me in the portfolio, like Sancho Panza between the bucklers, in the Island of Barataria, or she might have affixed the plate upon my head as the knight did Mambrino's helmet ; but this not occurring to her, I escaped with a good lecture and a pocket-handkerchief fastened to my frock, which, as it was quite clean, was scarcely perceptible. All this was meant for the benefit of the French dancing master ; but, alas ! poor " madame " was not aware that he was not coming till after supper, and that the intervening hour was devoted to standing upon one leg, like a goose upon a common, or to marching to the right and to the left, under the superintendence of a drill sergeant ! The man of war arrived. It is impossible to say whether the professor of marching or the poor Frenchwoman looked most disconcerted. The culprits unfortunately did not mind it at all. At length " madame " began a very voluble oration, intended to express the extent of our delinquency. But, alas ! " madame " was again unfortunate. How should a drill-sergeant understand French ! She was therefore driven to translate. " It is, sare, *que ces dames*—dat dese miss be ' *des traîneuses* ' " ; but this clear and intelligible sentence producing no other visible effect than a shake of the head, " madame " desired me (who happened to be next her) to tell him what she had said in English, and to tell her who *he* was. Did not my situation resemble that of Pistol's boy when he was ordered

to " construe " to M. Le Fer, that his master would
" fer, and ferret, and firk him " ? I had to find
English for " *traîneuses*," and French for drill-
sergeant. I, however, got over my difficulties by
calling him (by analogy) " *un maître de marche*,"
and telling him frankly that we were in disgrace.
The man was good-natured, and said we could not
possibly walk with all those incumbrances. There
could be no difficulty in translating that speech,
you know. So the gloves, the shawls, the music-
books, and the dictionaries were all taken off, and
we remained as before, only half-stifled with
suppressed laughter. Thus ended this experiment
in education, and thus ends my story.

I send you no compliments, my dear sir, not even
the compliments of the season, but the best good
wishes of our family circle, and particularly of her
who is ever

Most sincerely and affectionately yours,
MARY RUSSELL MITFORD.

To Sir William Elford, Bath

BERTRAM HOUSE, *Jan.* 28, 1812.

I will, my dear Sir William, even at the risk of
provoking you to think " good manners a desirable
accomplishment," plainly tell you that I believe
you to be quite mistaken in thinking that young
ladies are generally speaking good correspondents. As to experience, you and I are probably much upon an even footing. You have

not, perhaps, had much commerce with them ; neither have I.

I have lived so little with girls of my own age, and have been so much accustomed to think papa my pleasantest companion, and mamma my best friend, that, excepting with one dear and lovely cousin who is to me as a sister, and one most beloved friend (Losia Choynowska), from whom I am separated by the living death of immeasurable distance, I have escaped unscathed from all the charming folly and delectable romance of female intimacy and female confidence. I have, however, seen quite enough of the pretty letters of pretty ladies to let you into the whole art and mystery of epistolary trade ; and, relying upon you not to expose me as " an owl among the birds," I will, as far as in me lies, try to show you that it is really possible for you to write *passably*, though you have not the good fortune to be a young lady.

The first class of these fair correspondents is much the best. These are the apologizing damsels, who write once in three months ; whose letters regularly begin with " I am ashamed," and go on with various luminous and edifying excuses—such as the illness of a lap-dog or a third cousin, or a ball a month back, or a marriage that had been, or was to be, or that ought to have been and was not to be ; or a dress worked, or a trimming painted for the said marriage—and so you are fairly set down in the middle of the second page ; and just as the real letter is begun (for surely these preliminary excuses

are no part of a letter), the postman calls, or the
dinner-bell rings, and the disconsolate fair one, who
meant (yes, she certainly did mean it, for she tells
you so) to have written you a full sheet, is obliged to
" tear herself away with scarcely time to sign herself
your affectionate friend." Peace be to them, sweet
simpletons ! as unmeaning, as unvaried, and, thank
Heaven ! as brief as their own dinner-bells.

My next set consists of two apparently opposite
classes. The ladies in " issimo "—the setters up
and the pullers down—those to whom all is best,
or those to whom all is worst ; agreeing in nothing,
excepting in discharging upon their correspondents
the full glittering fountain of their happiness, or
the swollen muddy cascade of their discontent.
The first sort cannot go upon a water-party but
you must read an account of it in three full sheets.
All the dresses of all the ladies—all the speeches
of all the gentlemen—and all the songs sung by the
whole party—are the first described, the second
detailed, and the third copied for your amusement.
While every tree and hill, and stream and flower,
and weed and leaf, and the sun, moon, and stars,
and even the wind, and the clouds, come in for a
share of description or apostrophe ; though, indeed,
as Nature is much less to their taste than art, these
glorious objects generally escape with much less
notice than the colour of a pendant or the shape of a
saltcellar. The complainers are quite as tiresome,
and certainly more distressing. If they tell you
of a journey, you must expect to hear of " moving

accidents by flood and field." The weather is
always bad ; if there be but a cloud as big as a pin's
head, it descends in the form of a shower the
moment they have opened their carriage. They
are always overset in the dirtiest ways, and be-
nighted in the most dangerous places ; their horses
are always restive and their postilions always
drunken. The inns are dirty, the chambermaid
awkward, and the sheets damp ; and all these evils
fall with an unpitying hand on the devoted heads
of their correspondents.

But this is nothing to your sentimentalist. We
may have some pity for evils which, exaggerated as
they are, are yet real and tangible. But for the soft
distresses of a gentle damsel who is afraid that
another dear bosom friend (for these pretty creatures,
who cannot live without a sister soul, generally
manage to have a *corps de réserve*, in case of loss by
death, or marriage, or quarrels, or rivalry, or any
other unhappy accident) has looked coldly upon her,
or has neglected to return a pressure of the hand,
or has suffered twenty-four hours to pass without
answering her last note, or has committed some
other *crime de lèse-majesté* against the " inviolable
sanctity of their never-ending friendship," and begs
your advice and assistance in so dreadful a dilemma :

To laugh were want of goodness and of grace,
But to be grave exceeds all power of face.

One class more, and I have done. I mean your
learned young ladies—pedants in petticoats—who

are crammed from their infancy with languages, arts, and sciences, much in the same way that my good old nurse used to stuff bran into a pincushion. These *gentilles démoiselles* are the most perplexing of all. They mean to astonish, and they generally succeed. You cannot read their letters without a lexicon, nor understand them without an encyclopædia. As to their subjects, they reach from earth to heaven ; it is impossible to reckon them. They will write you a dissertation on the comet, or an explanation of the Portland vase—a *catalogue raisonné* of the British Museum, or a true account of the now extinct animals who sailed with Noah in the ark. But for the most part they talk of gases and galvanism, of columns and pilasters, and pistils and corolla ; quote Hebrew, and tell you they are just going to learn hydrostatics.

I so hate, myself, to have deductions and morals forced down my throat, that I make it a point of conscience not to torment you with them. I must, however, observe that in this educating age everything is taught to women except that which is perhaps worth all the rest—the power and the habit of thinking. Do not misunderstand me. I would not turn women into statesmen or philosophers. It is the privilege of man to govern, and the happiness of woman to obey. I would only wish that, while everything is invented and inculcated that can serve to amuse, to occupy, or adorn youth— youth which needs so little amusement or ornament !—something should be instilled that may add

pleasure and respectability to age. That bad letters
of every kind arise from want of the habit of thinking, I cannot doubt. There is, too, a yet deeper
evil : the little thought that is permitted, is directed
to very wrong objects—to dress and to matrimony—
both as a means and an end. They dress to marry
and marry to dress ; and so dressing and so marrying, there are, I fear, but small chances that they
will make good wives or good letter-writers.

Pray, my dear Sir William, have you ever had
occasion to see a great boaster thoroughly humbled ?
" And, pray, my dear madam, why do you ask me ? "
will be your reply. Read and you will know. A
little fat damsel, with whom you are sufficiently
acquainted to say—no ! I cry you mercy !—to
write very pretty things to, was till within this
fortnight a very great braggart. She knew, it is
true, that she was much subject to moral fear ; that
to be introduced to one whom she greatly admired
always gave her an ague fit ; and that to enter a
drawing-room full of company, unless she could
creep in behind her mamma, was worse than going
into a shower-bath—but then she thought to herself
(and sometimes I am afraid she said), " This is not
personal fear—this is shyness, not cowardice ; and
in personal danger I have no doubt but I should
have sufficient resolution ! "

Was not this sad boasting ? Though, to do the
poor girl justice, she had some reason for thinking
herself a heroine ; she never started or screamed at
spiders, frogs, snakes, or oxen ; she never either felt

or expressed any fears of being overset in a carriage
or robbed upon Hounslow Heath. She had once
been stranded in a man-of-war's boat on a sandbank
off St. Helen's, and had been obliged to wait the
return of the tide without a possibility of either
getting off to sea or making land, and in the midst
of scolding, sighing, crying, squalling, and sobbing,
she had felt neither pain nor fear, except of hunger ;
and *pour comble de courage*, she had actually slept
in an old castle in Northumberland which had once
had the reputation of being haunted, and neither
dreamt of spectres nor lay awake expecting a ghost
to pull back the curtains. Had she not a right
to think herself brave till she was proved a
coward ?

Now to my story. One night, about a fortnight
ago, this damsel was writing, as she often does,
about half-past eleven. Her mamma was reading ;
the men-servants were gone to bed ; and two silly
maids remained up frightening one another about
robberies and murders. All of a sudden a great
noise was heard at the back door—a noise of shouting, knocking, and bouncing ; and the silly maids,
instead of answering to the loud and repeated
demands for entrance, ran upstairs to their mistresses
to assure them that they were certainly going to be
robbed and murdered. What effect this comfortable intelligence might have had I know not.

All the passions are contagious, and none, perhaps, so catching as fear. But do not think that
their report would have alarmed the subject (I wish

I could say the heroine) of my tale, had it not been
accompanied by a most fearful repetition of the
shouting, knocking, and bouncing at the *front* door !
This was really terrible.   One maiden volunteered
to put her head half out of the study door, which
was open, to listen ; and she declared there was a
whole army of them, all " men in buckram and men
in Kendal green, and it was so dark you could not
see the back of your hand."   The mamma was not
at all frightened, but the daughter followed the
other damsels up the back-stairs to call up their
natural defenders, the men ; and there she stood
midway, leaning upon the bannisters and listening
to a repetition of fearful dreams and bloody omens
—till she was reinforced by one valiant man, and
roused to some exertion by hearing that the other,
" a great lubberly boy " of seventeen, had declared
that if he must die, he certainly would die in his
bed.

You cannot think how much good the being
obliged to scream and scold him through the door
did her ; and whether the eloquence of fear or the
being fairly dragged out of bed by one of the
frightened maids prevailed, he certainly did get up,
and the whole cavalcade—much cheered by finding
that as the knocking still continued, and the cour-
ageous man-servant had proceeded with a gun to
the post of danger, they at least should not die un-
avenged—prepared to descend.   It was truly edifying to observe the respect of the servants and the
humility of the young lady ; they would not for

the world go before her ; and she condescended
to walk down the back-stairs. By the time they
had got half-way down—for the procession moved
with dignified slowness and solemnity—they heard
sounds extremely different from those which had
alarmed them ; sounds which could not be mistaken, for they were those of mirth and laughter.
And the terrible robbers and murderers, " the men
in buckram " and " the men in Kendal green,"
proved to be one poor solitary messenger, who had
brought a parcel from the Reading coach office, and,
having been called out of his bed and lost his way,
had fancied the family must be in bed and asleep
too, and that he and his horse had nothing for it
but to make as much noise as would, I think, have
awakened the seven sleepers.

I must not, however, make the worst of a bad
story. Your little friend neither sobbed, nor wept,
nor fainted : she only trembled a little and lost her
colour for the first time of her life ; and she
recovered so soon, that she was able to correct a
very incorrect proof of a certain *Ode to Genius*
which the messenger brought and took back again,
and to write to her dear papa, and even to finish
the intricate machinery of a Spenser stanza, in
which she was engaged when the alarm began,
before she went to bed. *À propos* of the *Ode to
Genius*, I am delighted that you like it, not only
because I am always proud of your approbation, but
because—it looks very vain to say so, but as it is the
first time that it has happened with anything that I

have written—I really like it myself. And I hear that it is much spoken of in London.

I most sincerely hope that we shall meet this spring in London, where we should have been long ago had not the purchaser of this place been a righteous, canting, cheating London upholsterer, who, having already three houses, found out after buying this that it was one too many, and has been trying to get rid of a bargain much too advantageous to him, by starting frivolous objections against a title which is, I believe, as clear as anything can be which has been handled by lawyers. This it is which has occasioned a delay extremely incon-venient, as we had packed up most of our things, dismissed several of our servants, and have been for the last five months ready to set out at a week's warning. I now hope that things are coming to a crisis, and that by April or May we shall have the pleasure of renewing (I might almost say com-mencing) our personal acquaintance. You will find just the same plain, awkward, blushing thing whom you profess to remember ; only I think the almost hermit life that I have led for the last year has rather improved all these enchanting qualifications. I talk to you with wonderful boldness upon paper, and while we are seventy miles distant ; but I doubt whether I shall say three sentences to you when we meet, because the ghosts of all my impertinent letters will stare me in the face the moment I see you. Where I got all this bashfulness, Heaven only knows ! Papa, indeed, says I inherit it from

him. He is now in town. Mamma desires me
to give her best respects, and I beg you to
believe me,

Very sincerely and affectionately yours,

MARY RUSSELL MITFORD.

To Sir William Elford, Graham Club,
St. James's Street

BERTRAM HOUSE, *April* 5, 1812.

My father and mother are in Hampshire, and I
am just returned from one of those field rambles
which in the first balmy days of spring are so enchanting. And yet the meadows, in which I have
been walking, are nothing less than picturesque.
To a painter they would offer no attraction—to a
poet they would want none. Read and judge for
yourself in both capacities. It is a meadow, or
rather a long string of meadows, irregularly divided
by a shallow winding stream, swollen by the late
rains to unusual beauty, and bounded on the one
side by a ragged copse, of which the outline is
perpetually broken by sheep walks and more beaten
paths, which here and there admit a glimpse of low
white cottages, and on the other by tall hedgerows,
abounding in timber, and strewn like a carpet with
white violets, primroses, and oxlips. Except that
occasionally over the simple gates you catch a view
of the soft and woody valleys, the village churches
and the fine seats which distinguish this part of
Berkshire, excepting this short and unfrequent

peep at the world, you seem quite shut into these smiling meads.

Oh how beautiful they were to-day, with all their train of callow goslings and frisking lambs and laughing children chasing the butterflies that floated like animated flowers in the air, or hunting for birds' nests among the golden-blossomed furze ! How full of fragrance and of melody ! It is when walking in such scenes, listening to the mingled notes of a thousand birds, and inhaling the mingled perfume of a thousand flowers, that I feel the real joy of existence. To live ; to share with the birds and the insects the delights of this beautiful world ; to have the mere consciousness of *being*, is happiness. You see how full the cup of joy is to-day that it runs over. If I was ever guided by any other motive than the feeling of the moment in writing to you, I certainly should not have chosen this time to send you a specimen of my rural enthusiasm, which you will receive in an atmosphere where enthusiasm cannot breathe—in the gay bustle of St. James's Street.

It is well for me that I can plead privilege (the privilege of gentle poesy) for my madness ; or you might perhaps, out of friendship for papa, send down Dr. Willis and a strait waistcoat, or exert yourself to gain me an admission to St. Luke's. " Vastly well, madam ! I forgive your description —I admit your apology—I know your privilege ; but what is all this to my white moss roses ? " My dear Sir William, be patient. " Patience is a virtue," was my writing-master's favourite copy. (I really had a writing-master, whatever you may think of the matter.) Be patient, and you shall hear—that just at present I can tell you nothing about them. This, you know, is Sunday ; and even if I could get to Reading (which, till the return of our equipage, a most commodious dog-cart, I cannot do), the worthy seedsman, Mr. Swallow, who adds to his other occupations that of spiritual teacher to a vast congregation of Methodists, certainly would not let me even look at his roses. I do not suppose he would even let the roses blow if he could help it. But to-morrow will be Monday ; and to-morrow your faithful subjects William Swallow, and George Mitford, and Mary Russell Mitford, and the dog-cart, and the white moss roses (if any such there be, for I never heard of them), and the yellow roses will meet together, and exert themselves in their several capacities to obey your royal mandate.

To Sir William Elford, 18 *Bury Street, St. James's*

BERTRAM HOUSE, *April* 22, 1812.

I am highly flattered, my dear Sir William, to find that you think my letters worth preserving. I keep yours as choice as the monks were wont to keep the relics of their saints ; and about sixty years hence your grandson or great-grandson will discover in the family archives some notice of such a collection, and will send to the grandson of my dear

cousin Mary (for as I intend to die an old maid, I
shall make her heiress to all my property, *i.e.* my
MSS.) for these inestimable remains of his venerable ancestor. And then, you know, my letters
will be rummaged out, and the whole correspondence will be sorted and transcribed, and sent to
the press, adorned with portraits, and *facsimiles*,
and illustrated by lives of the authors, beginning
with the register of their births, and ending with
their epitaphs. Then it will come forth into the
world, and set all the men a-crowing and talking
over their old nonsense (with more show of reason,
however, than ordinary) about the superiority of
the sex. What a fine job the transcriber of my
letters will have ! I hope the booksellers of those
days will be liberal and allow the poor man a good
price for his trouble ; no one but an unraveller of
state cyphers can possibly accomplish it.

What you say respecting my choice of flowers
only proves that your taste is as humble as mine.
But I do assure you that a jury of florists would give
a verdict against us for bad taste in any country in
Christendom. Why, here is my dear mamma,
watching with careful eyes the unfolding of a
magnificent camellia japonica, and here is our good
neighbour, Mrs. Reeve (ah ! ah ! fair lady ! I will
teach you to steal into a room and look over my
shoulder !)—here is Mrs. Reeve who ought to love
what she so much resembles, and yet cannot endure
the sight of a rose, except those which her gardener
brings in February and March from her hot-house

to her drawing-room ; poor sickly flowers, which have never been fanned by the air of heaven, nor refreshed by any showers but those from a watering-pot. Ask either of these ladies (especially the last, for mamma loves all that is good and all that is beautiful, whether in a field or a garden, a cottage window or a drawing-room) what flowers they admire, and they will answer you by a thousand unspeakable names of bulbs from Caffraria, and shrubs from the American mountains. For my part, I am delighted at this coincidence of taste between us. I place flowers in the very first rank of simple pleasures ; and I have no very good opinion of the hard worldly people who take no delight in them.

WHITLEY COTTAGE, *Friday*.

Did you ever happen to write with a pen twenty years old, and just a drop and a half of ink, in the midst of a universal clackit of female tongues ? If you never did, you are no competent judge of my present situation, and to describe it is impossible. Who can describe the almost inconceivable *mélange* of a true female gossip ; where dress and music, dancing and preaching, pelisses and beaux, flowers and scandal, all meet together, like the oil and vinegar of a salad ? It must, however, plead my apology for all blunders.

How short a time you stay in London this year ! Not even to see the Exhibition open, though you will of course see it with the rest of the great people before it is opened to the public. Have you a picture there this year ?

Adieu, my dear sir. Mamma desires her best respects.

Ever most sincerely and affectionately yours,

                                    MARY RUSSELL MITFORD.

To Sir William Elford, Bickham, Plymouth

BERTRAM HOUSE, *July* 1, 1812.

Thanks be to your Plymouth electors, and to Colonel Bloomfield, and to you, and to all the causes and agents concerned in your franking promise. Not because it saves my purse, although that is of course properly light and poetical, but because it gives me a charming prospect of a double portion of sense and wit from " my dear, and good, and kind correspondent."

To say that I anticipate with delight every book of Miss Edgeworth's is but to re-echo the opinion of all the world ; but I must do my own taste the justice to say that I delight in her works for the same reason that you admire them—her exquisite distinction of character ; whereas I am convinced that at least nine-tenths of her readers are caught solely by the humour of her dialogue and the liveliness of her illustrations—the mere costume and drapery of her enchanting pictures. I am not, however, sure that I shall like *Anne of Brittany* the better for being historical. I never read an historical novel in my life that I did not exchange my little previous knowledge of the period and characters referred to, for the falsified events and imaginary personages of the novelist ; and in spite of Sir Robert Walpole's notion of history, I am by no means certain that the change is in my favour. And yet this strange aberration of memory is as natural as it is humiliating. There is something so delightful in the idea of penetrating into the minds and motives of those heroes and statesmen of whom the historian tells us nothing but the actions ; something so attractive in seeing the warrior softened—not degraded—into humanity and partaking of our wants, our wishes, and our hopes, that we lend ourselves willingly to the delusion, and are contented to resign the meagre outline of Hume for the brilliant colouring of Miss Porter. It is this which renders Shakespeare's historical plays so infinitely interesting, in defiance of Aristotle and Voltaire.

By-the-way, when we were abusing Kemble, I wonder (only I believe that I was a little *dashed*) that I did not tell you that I have a theory respecting play-writing and play-acting which Shakespeare certainly, and I think Garrick, contrived to realize. It does appear to me that no man can be a perfect tragedian who is not likewise a good actor in the higher branch of comedy. A statesman not at the council board, and a hero when the battle is safely ended, would, as it seems to me, talk and walk much in the same way with other people. Even a tyrant does not always rave, nor a lover always whine. A king may order his horse without a start, and a misanthrope talk of the weather without a groan.

Now, Messrs. Kemble and Co. never do converse —they always declaim, and that not in the very best manner ; so that between long pauses and unnatural cadences, the audience have nothing for it but to fall asleep and dream of Shakespeare. That he and all the writers of Elizabeth's days (the real Augustan age of English poetry) were of my opinion, I am quite sure. Nothing is more remarkable in their delightful dramas, especially in those of Ford, Massinger, and Fletcher, than the sweet and natural tone of conversation which sometimes relieves the terrible intensity of their plots like a flowery glade in a gloomy forest, or a sunbeam streaming up a winter sky. I hope you give me credit for proving that my theory (unlike most modern theories) is practicable, by deducing it from the actual practice of our poets. I cannot take leave of the drama without adding my feeble tribute of regret for the secession of Mrs. Siddons. Yet it was better that she should quit the stage in undiminished splendour than have remained to show the feeble twilight of so glorious a day. Tragedy, poor Tragedy ! must now fly from her superb arena and take shelter in the pages of Shakespeare and the bosom of Miss Baillie.

Have your maiden-blush moss roses and your yellow roses blown yet ? My yellow roses are all eaten this year by some abominable insect with which you, as a naturalist, have probably the honour of being acquainted. Not one rose have I been able to save. So much the worse for my good friend Mrs. Monck ; for, as I can't do without them, I go to Coley Park and steal hers. You can't conceive what a thief I am in my heart. I went to Lord Rivers's the other day to see his stud, and I was seized with a prodigious inclination to steal near a hundred greyhounds. Luckily, however, I recollected that, if I stole the greyhounds, I must likewise steal the keepers ; and, if I stole the keepers, I must steal the house and kennels ; and, if I stole the house and kennels, I must steal money to keep them, which might, you know, have certain consequences not very agreeable. So I actually came away without stealing, and, what is still more extraordinary, without even begging a greyhound puppy. I have been thinking what I had to say to you, but I cannot think, because the room is so distressingly quiet. Mamma is at work, and papa (who I verily believe fancies I am composing an epic poem) has taken up a book, not to interrupt me. Now nothing is to me so *fidgeting* (forgive this female word) as silence. Dryden has been much laughed at for a line of his—

A horrid stillness now invades the ear,—

which Johnson (I think) defended upon the ground that stillness, like darkness, is privation, and that the personification is allowable. I should have defended it, too, for a different reason. Is there such a thing as perfect stillness—as an entire absence

of all sound ?   I think not.   It appears to me that
what we call stillness is, in fact, only a substitution
of lower for louder sounds.   I do not, indeed, hear
my dear father's cheerful voice ; but I can hear the
rain dropping on the skylight, the wind jarring the
doors, the turning over the leaves of the book, nay
even the very movement of mamma's quick-passing
needle ; and I think you will agree with me that
" point," " quint " and " quatorze," the triumphs
and even the murmurings of picquet, were preferable to this unquiet stillness.   I fear, too, that you
will agree with what I know mamma thinks, that
it is time to say good-night, and go to bed.   You do
not like naughty children, I know ; so I will only
stay to present my dear, dear parents' kindest
remembrances.   Good-night and pleasant dreams,
my dear friend !

Ever most sincerely and affectionately yours,

MARY RUSSELL MITFORD.

To Sir William Elford

BERTRAM HOUSE, *Oct.* 27, 1812.

The echoing Town Hall is at length empty—the
din of tongues is at an end—the well-fee'd lawyers
have ceased to browbeat or to cajole—their unhappy
clients have for a short space forgotten to murmur
—the stealers of chickens and pilferers of corn-
sheaves, the reluctant menders of bad roads, and
the still more reluctant wedders of disconsolate
damsels—some in the friendly clutch of the gaoler,

some in the still harder grasp of the parish officer—
have taken their departure ; and the bench itself,
with all its precious lumber, the simpering simpletons who talk nonsense in its original form of silly
frivolity, and the solemn coxcombs who talk the far
worse nonsense which looks like dull sense, have
at length retired to forget their fatigues in port and
politics.   In a word, the first day of the Quarter
Sessions is ended, and my father informs me that
to-morrow will be an excellent opportunity to
initiate some of the new members into the use of the
only privilege which I was ever disposed to envy
them—to frank this letter.

I am afraid—but pray don't tell of my misfortune
—that to my unfashionable organs the exquisite
variety of Dryden is more agreeable than the uniform sweetness of Pope.   I hope you do not suspect
me of comparing Pope to Miss Seward ; though I
must confess that I did often compare her letters
(while reading them, with pleasure, with curiosity,
but without one spark of respect or affection) with
that enchanting Madame de Sévigné, whom one is
tempted to adore—with that amiable Cowper,
whom it is impossible not to love—and with that
delightful Lord Orford, who forces one at will to
laugh and to admire.   À *propos* to Lord Orford,
I have just been reminded of a letter of his, in which
he describes Netley Abbey, with its beautiful
surrounding scenery, in nearly the same point of
view in which I attempted to delineate it.[1]

[1] In a poem called ' Weston.'

You are right in supposing Mr. Chamberlayne to be the gentleman who will succeed to the great Dummer property at the death of Lady Holland. Netley Abbey forms a part of this demesne ; and I suppose its vicinity to the large estate, of which he has so near a prospect, was one reason, joined to its almost unrivalled situation, for his fixing on Weston Grove for the site of his fairy palace. If he had not spent all his treasures, as he says, in this election contest (the deuce take election contests ! You are the only wise man of my acquaintance, for being absolutely proof against temptation), he and Dr. Parr and Mr. Fox and I (a very pretty quartetto !) should all have cut a resplendent figure in stone and on paper ; for he, Mr. Chamberlayne, meant to have erected a column to the memory of Mr. Fox, " now that it seems forgotten by princes and people," and Dr. Parr had written a beautiful Latin inscription for the said column, and you cannot doubt (at least you must make-believe that there can be no doubt about it) that I should have composed an equally beautiful *éloge* on the object in vulgar English. I should indeed have written *con amore* ; and yet, with all due deference to Dr. Parr and to politics, I am not sure that, if I were to erect a column to Mr. Fox I would not sooner inscribe it with that one sweet sentence of Gibbon's, which you must remember as well as I, than with all the Latin that ever was written in the world.

You will forgive me for my idolatry with regard

to Fox, and I will forgive you for your " *Belle Démocrate*," and your saucy and inconsistent insinuation that I, the said *Démocrate*, am a well-wisher to Napoleon, the greatest enemy to Democracy that ever existed. I will not pretend to prophesy how he may escape from his " Moscow grid-iron " ; but I am afraid, greatly afraid, that he who has a trick of finding resources where no one else would dream of looking for them, will not be so easily vanquished as our ministers and the magnanimous Alexander appear to anticipate. Most sincerely do I wish that he may be entangled in inextricable difficulties, for then I should hope that we, that England, that the world might have some chance for the only political object which seems to me worth a wish or a prayer—that this dreadful, this exterminating contest, might at length terminate in peace. I show some confidence in your good opinion when I dare to tell you—without fearing to incur the suspicion of being a mere namby-pamby miss, striving to look amiable—that peace ! peace ! peace ! is my political creed. Oh, my dear sir, lose for a moment that feeling of habit of familiarity with blood, by which we are apt, reversing more madly the mad error of Don Quixote, to look upon armies as flocks of sheep prepared for their necessary slaughter ; reflect that they are men, treading upon the same earth, breathing the same air, endowed with the same faculties, the same feelings, the same affections as ourselves ; bound, too, by the same ties of social sympathy and of natural

connections ; and then view them dead, dying,
mangled in the field of battle, or burning with their
wives and children amid their smoking habitations :
think that all this may happen on English ground ;
and then support war if you can.

I care not who makes peace, whether Lord Grey,
Lord Castlereagh, or Sir Francis Burdett, or what
be the party watchword, whether the silly cry of
" No Popery," or the equally silly one of " Catholic
Emancipation " ; let us have peace ; and our sinful
nation will be at once absolved from half her crimes.
I know not how you will pardon me for having thus
intruded on you a woman's politics, though you
partly drew the evil upon yourself.   I can only promise to offend so no more, and have recourse to your
section of a jerk [1]—(" I thank thee, Jew, for teaching
me that word ")—to obliterate the remembrance.

Pray, my dear friend, have you read the little
volume of *Rejected Addresses* ? If you have not,
you positively must. It is absolutely delightful !
and it is extremely magnanimous in me to think
and to say so ; for the author has contrived to
affront me in the tenderest point—not my verses ;
there, thank Heaven ! my happy insignificance
protected me—but in my *name*. If there was one
thing in which I took a pride, it was in that old
respectable name of mine. It was such a comfort
to be neither Short nor Long, nor White nor Brown,
nor Green nor Black, to belong to no streets or

[1] A jerk was the name that Sir W. Elford gave to the wavy
line, ∽ , used to indicate a change of subject.

alleys—to have nothing to do with the vulgar tribes of Jackson, Robson, Dobson, or Gilbertson—to appertain, in short, to the genteel family of the " fords," and carry the mark of Domesday Book upon one's very tickets.

Well, my dear Sir William, what do you think this wicked wit of a writer has taken it into his head to do.? He has actually introduced this dearly-beloved name of " Mitford " (which I mean to keep, nevertheless) as belonging to a fireman, among a heap of Muggins's and Huggins's and Scroggins's and Higginbottoms, in a parody upon Walter Scott !   And what do you think may be the appellation of this impertinent ?   " Oh ! Howard, or Percy, or Clifford, or Devereux, or Scrope." No; it is neither.   His name is one compared to which the Whites, the Browns, the Shorts, the Greens, the Streets, and the Jacksons are elegant and un-common ; his name is neither more nor less than Smith !—James Smith, attorney-at-law in the good city of London ! After all, he is so clever, that I must forgive him. I am not sure that I do not like the prose addresses, Cobbett's and Johnson's, better than the verse ; though Fitzgerald's loyal effusion, the whole of Wordsworth's, and part of Southey's, Coleridge's, and Scott's are admirable for the nice imitation of style which is intermixed with the broad burlesque.

Adieu, my dear sir.

Your sincere and affectionate friend,
MARY RUSSELL MITFORD.

To Sir William Elford, Bickham, Plymouth

BERTRAM HOUSE, *Dec.* 13, 1812.

I sit down, my dear Sir William, to tell you, as well as I can, what I think of *Clarissa*. It is some years since I read it, and even then I skipped a good part of it ; but it is one of those works which it is impossible ever to forget, because it stamps itself, not on the memory, but the heart. What a genius had Richardson ! With every fault of style, of plot, of subject, which a writer could have—with the most wearying repetitions, the most distressing coarseness of painting—with characters the most abhorrent to our feelings, and scenes the most repugnant to our delicacy—he has yet contrived to enchain our every thought and passion : and this he has effected by his angelic heroine, and by her alone. Clarissa was from first to last the sole object which inspired me with any, the smallest degree, of interest and affection ; and I am not sure (so malicious am I) whether I was not almost as much pleased with the earthly punishment of the Har-lowes—that detestable race !—as with the beatifica-tion of their sainted daughter. You see that I do not agree with those critics who object to the character of Lovelace as too agreeable. Agreeable, truly ! I am not sure that Solmes is not the more bearable animal of the two. The fault in my opinion is *vice versa*. Lovelace is now so degraded by his vices that Clarissa could not have loved him without degradation ; and, accordingly, we see very plainly that she does not love him. She is not led by affection, but driven by fear into his toils.

If Richardson could have drawn an amiable man (which he took care to show that he could not by writing *Sir Charles Grandison*), it would much have added both to the moral and pathetic effect, to have represented her affections as deeply engaged to Lovelace. Tell me, my dear friend, why is it so much easier to draw a fine female character than an interesting and excellent man ? Richardson himself has Clarissa, Clementina, Emily (I don't reckon Harriet Byron, because I don't like her), and not one producible man to set against them. Miss Edgeworth is nearly in the same predicament ; so are Charlotte Smith and Miss Burney. Indeed, I scarcely know one *héros de roman*, whom it is possible to admire, except Wallace in Miss Porter's *Scottish Chiefs*.

À propos of criticism, I was lately looking over the poems of an old friend of my father's, Mr. Thomas Warton (the laureate), and I there found, to my great astonishment, an ode which I should, from internal evidence, have pronounced at once to have been written by Walter Scott. It is called " The Grave of King Arthur." Read it ; it is well worth looking for. Read it, and you will find there all the peculiarities and all the beauties of the Border Minstrel—his locality, his chivalry, his versification, and his style. You will there find too, or I am much mistaken, the very ideas and imagery of the finest part of *The Lay*, Deloraine's visit to Melrose ; and, if you are fond of comparative criticism, you will be amused to trace the *décadence* from the grand and sublime agents and objects of Warton, his King Henry and King Arthur, with the gigantic armour and the gifted Kaliburn, to the old dead wizard, the moss trooper, and the Book of Choice Magical Receipts of Walter Scott. Oh, how much he has lowered it ! You will find, too, the first draught of the minstrel ;— and all this vast source of imitation is comprised in an ode of four pages ! What would the critics, who accuse me of imitating Mr. Scott, say, if *I* did so ? They will soon have an opportunity to admonish again, for *Blanch* is out—out and I have not sent her to you ! The truth is, my dear Sir William, that there are situations in which it is a duty to give up all expensive luxuries, even the luxury of offering the little tribute of gratitude and friendship ; and I had no means of restraining papa from scattering my worthless book all about to friends and foes, but by tying up my own hands from presenting any, except to two or three very near relations. I have told you all this because I am not ashamed of being poor, and because perfect frankness is in all cases the most pleasant as well as the most honourable to both parties.

I must now bid you adieu, my dear friend, though my letter may probably wait a few days for a frank. Pray let me hear soon. We all join in best wishes for many happy years to you and yours.

Ever most gratefully and affectionately yours,

M. R. M.

To Sir William Elford, Bath

BERTRAM HOUSE, *Dec.* 31, 1812.

MY DEAR SIR WILLIAM,

I won't detain you with any comments upon your mistake with regard to my affection for Lord Grey, against whom I happen to have a very particular spleen, but pass on at once to *Clarissa*, the grand object of your last delightful letter. Nothing in the world can stand against your wit, when you choose to make use of that powerful artillery ; therefore I—having made battle as long as I possibly could for that " Champion of Dames," Mr. Richardson—shall certainly think proper to capitulate at discretion ; or (to lower my metaphor a little) having defended my master's meat from your attacks as long as possible, I shall e'en sit quietly down and pick a bit with you. I quite agree with you as to the Harlowes, young and old ; the vile and improbable plot ; the disgusting means by which it is brought about ; and the abominable folly, or worse than folly, of supposing chastity anything extraordinary ; and I am not quite sure that I do not partly agree with you as to Clarissa's character. If she had been as prosperous as Sir Charles Grandison she would have been as insupportable ; as it is, her piety, her resignation, her mental chastity throw a veil over all but her virtues.

I once knew a little of a lady who professed to make Clarissa her rule of life. She was, as you may imagine, a mere piece of clockwork ; said her prayers, ordered dinner, walked, talked, read good books, and scolded the servants to the instant. I dare say she could have set the sun, if he had happened to go astray in his declination. This good lady was, to the unspeakable misery of all concerned, a wife and a mother ; but of all human beings she had most decidedly the outward and visible marks of " ancient virginity." Hogarth's " Old Maid of a Frosty Morning " was the image of her, mind and body. As to Sir Charles Grandison himself, he is a man of marble, or rather a man of snow ; just like the companions of Laila in Mr. Southey's *Thalaba*—snow-people, who walk and talk, and eat and drink, and do everything but feel ; and yet this composition of frost is always deploring his unfortunate sensibility ! If I had lived in those days and been honoured by his acquaintance, I should certainly have been minded to give him a hearty pinch, to find whether he really was made of flesh and blood ; or to bend him up and down, to discover whether he had a poker driven through him. That Sir Charles is really my horror. And yet the thing the most approaching to nature in all Richardson (at least in all that I have read of him, for *Pamela* I have never seen) is the character of Emily Jervois in that very book. I like her better

than Clementina, whom the worthy author chose
to degrade so unnecessarily by first of all making her
follow that bewitching snow-man to England, and
then give a sort of promise to marry that other stick
of Italian growth, the Count of Belvedere.   Her
only proper place of refuge was a nunnery.

Perhaps I am not sufficiently versed in the
symptoms of madness, but I must confess Dr.
Warton's praise of Clementina, in his delightful
Commonplace Book on Pope, has always appeared
to me greatly exaggerated.   How is it possible to
compare it with the touching frenzy of Lear, where
every word goes so directly to the heart of every
one endued with human feeling ?

God bless you, my dear and ever-kind friend !   I
believe I may now wish to you and to all you love a
happy new year and many of them.

Your obliged and affectionate

M. R. MITFORD.

To Sir William Elford, Bickham

BERTRAM HOUSE, April 11, 1813.

I did not ask you to *send* me your pamphlet, my
dear friend ; I asked you to *bring* it.   And now,
since I must be a desolate, despairing damsel during
the whole year, and stroll about the fields shedding
melodious tears for the absence of my faithful
lovyer, I must even go to London and get it myself.
I can procure it at Longman's.

Talking of Longman's, I must tell you how citizen

booksellers feed dogs. One of the partners (Mr.
Rees) in that Leviathan firm made some time since
a most earnest application to papa for a cast greyhound, anything would do ; but he had passed a
week in Ettrick Forest with Walter Scott, who took
him out coursing every day, and he must have a
greyhound. Papa promised to consider the case,
came home, told me the story, and forgot it. It
so happened, however, towards the end of the
season, that he had a most beautiful young dog,
excellently well bred, in the highest condition, very
playful and affectionate, with only one fault in the
world—he could not run. I do verily believe had
he been destined to catch a mouse, in fair running
the mouse would have beaten him. What was to
be done with poor Madoc ? for so, an' please ye,
he was called. He was a beautiful picture, but as a
greyhound he was worse than as a picture ; for
there he had two faults—he ate and he was taxed.
" I 'll send him to Paternoster Row," said papa—
and to Paternoster Row he was sent. In spite of
his faults, poor Madoc was a favourite of mine, and
when papa went to town I begged him to call and
see him. He did so, and was immediately conducted into one of the warerooms, where Madoc,
on a whole truss of straw, had taken the place of
lumber much duller than himself—of Scotch meta-
physics, of Grub Street poetry, and of politics from
the King's Bench. There he sat in state, with a
huge platter containing all the odds and ends of the
kitchen, a sort of *olla podrida* of beef, mutton, and

veal, on one side of him, and an immense pan of
pease soup on the other. If Mr. Rees should ever
chance to discover that he cannot run, I design to
lay the fault entirely on this pease soup.

Is not Mr. C—— a Reformer ? How catching
is that talk about Reform ! It so flatters one's
vanity, to set about mending the State. It looks
so much wiser to find fault than to praise ; and it
is so much easier to boot ! Then, though one only
takes one's arguments from the last newspaper, all
hearers, from courtesy or fellow-feeling, give one
credit for originality ; and many persons, to my
certain knowledge, have got a very pretty sort of
country reputation for cleverness, from no other
source ; whilst, as is well known, you, the opposers
of innovation, never condescend to argue at all.
In short, to say nothing of the better enthusiasm
which the very sounds of purity and freedom never
fail to excite in the breasts of the young and ardent,
there are so many paltry passions and petty vanities
which one dignifies by the name of love of reform,
that I must end as I began, with saying that I
scarcely know whether I am a Reformer or not.
One thing is certain, if not a Reformer I am nothing ;
for I have as pretty a contempt for the ministers as
my whiggish papa ; and as comfortable a dislike
to the Whigs as my ministerial uncle.

What shall we talk of now ? Of something as
opposite to politics as night to day, or as music to
discord ; we will talk of the nightingales. They
are not come yet, though this warm weather would

certainly have brought them, if I had not sent to put them off till we had the happiness of seeing you. Now that I have no hopes of this pleasure I shall write them an invitation directly. I am not like Mrs. Opie's Glenmurray ; I can eat grapes if I can't get pineapple. Besides which I want the nightingales to console me. I shall not hear many of their sweet notes this year ; for when papa, who is now in London, returns home, he will take me almost immediately back with him to fulfil my engagements in town and the neighbourhood. Dear mamma, who is quite well again, Heaven be thanked, will remain here, and here you will be so good as to direct your next letter, because I am going to more than one house, and am not yet certain whether I shall first proceed to Tavistock House, to Mrs. Perry, or to Fulham, to Mrs. Wilson. Good-night, and God bless you !

Ever affectionately yours,

M. R. Mitford.

To Sir William Elford, Bickham

BERTRAM HOUSE, *June* 27, 1813.

Am I not better than good, my dear friend, to answer so soon ? After all your hard names too ; calling me " Echo " and " Jacobite," and God knows what ! If it had not been for the " Mary " in the conclusion I should certainly have broken my heart. It is very true that I have been running about more than usual this spring—first of all for

a month in town, and since at the house of a friend
in the forest for Ascot races ; but it is equally true
that I told you mamma would remain here, and
forward any letter from you, my dear, lazy, delightful correspondent.

I take it for granted that you are acquainted with
Mr. Moore, that " abridgment of all that is
pleasant in man." I never saw him till this spring,
when he dined frequently at Tavistock House.[1] I
am quite enchanted with him. He has got a little
wife (whom I did not see), and two little children,
and they are just gone into Wales, where he intends
to finish a great poem on which he is occupied. It
is a Persian tale, and he says it will be his fault if it
is not a fine work, for the images, the scenery, the
subject, are poetry itself. How his imagination
will revel among the roses, and the nightingales,
and the light-footed Almé !

I saw Mrs. Opie only once during my stay in
town, though we afterwards exchanged calls without
meeting. She looks, I think, very ill—thinner,
paler, and much older, but was, as she always is,
very kind and pleasant. I saw something else, too,
that reminded me of my dear Sir William. It was
not your pamphlet, which for want of going into
The Row, and a proper title to send for it by, I did
not see ; but your beautiful landscape, well placed
and looking to much advantage in the great room
of the Exhibition. I thought the paintings this
year extremely good, especially Wilkie's ' Blind-

[1] Mr. Perry's, Editor of the *Morning Chronicle*.

man's Buff" and Turner's "Frosty Morning";
but everything was thrown into the background by
Sir Joshua's exhibition. Though even there I was
partially disappointed—not in the general effect,
but in some of the cried-up pictures. What, for
instance, can be so uninspired as the celebrated
portrait of Mrs. Sheridan as St. Cecilia? The
"Death of Cardinal Beaufort" by no means
answered my expectations. There are some scenes
in poetry which painting had better let alone; and
this is one of them. It seems to me, too, that the
painter has mistaken his moment. "Lord Cardinal,
if thou think'st on Heaven's bliss, hold up thy
hand"—make signal of thy hope: "He dies, and
makes no sign." Now the expression indicated by
these words is despair—chill, hopeless, fixed despair;
whilst in the countenance of the picture nothing
can be traced but the contortions of bodily pain.
It is very impertinent in me, who know nothing of
painting, to make these observations to any one—
especially to you, who know so much.

Papa is in town, but he will, I am sure, and so
shall I, be delighted with your work on natural
history.

My dear mamma is quite well, and desires her
kindest compliments.

Ever, my dear sir,

Your obliged and affectionate friend,

M. R. M.

To Sir William Elford, Bickham, Plymouth

BERTRAM HOUSE, *Nov.* 10, 1813.

The occasion of this present infliction, my dear friend, proceeds from my desire to vent on some *sympathetic soul*, some *kindred spirit*, three feelings with which I am at present brim-full—admiration, anger, and perplexity. In the first I am sure you will sympathize most cordially, for it is excited by Burns—by Burns, the sweetest, the sublimest, the most tricksy poet who has blest this nether world since the days of Shakespeare ! I am just fresh from reading Dr. Currie's four volumes and Cromek's one, which comprise, I believe, all that he ever wrote ; and I cannot imagine how I can have wasted my admiration on the little living, and disregarded the mighty dead in the way that I have hitherto done. To make it worse, I had read Dr. Currie's *Life of Burns* before, when I was about twelve or thirteen, and yet I had almost forgotten him. If I forget him again " may my right hand forget its cunning " ! Have you lately read that delightful work ? If you have not, pray do, and tell me if you do not admire him—not with the flimsy, lackadaisical praise with which certain gentle damsels bedaub his " Mountain Daisy " and his " Woodlark," and talk and sing of the rustic bard as the compeer of Bloomfield,[1] and Stephen Duck,

[1] Robert Bloomfield, author of *The Farmer's Boy*, was the son of a village tailor, and died in poverty, before he had time to go mad. Stephen Duck was a thresher who wrote verses, became a beef-eater, was afterwards ordained, and, by the

and Mrs. Leapor ; but with the strong and manly
feeling which his fine and indignant letters, his
exquisite and original humour, his inimitable
pathos, must awaken in such a mind as yours. Oh,
what have they to answer for who let such a man
perish ! I think there is no poet whose works I
have ever read, who interests one so strongly by the
display of personal character contained in almost
everything he wrote (even in his songs) as Burns.
Those songs are for the greater part nearly his best
productions ; the very best is undoubtedly " Tam
o' Shanter." The humour, the grandeur, and the
fancy of that poem will never be equalled. What
a pity it is that Burns did not follow the advice of
my late excellent correspondent and adviser, Lord
Woodhouselee, and give the world some more tales
on that model ! His versatility and his exhaustless
imagination would have made it easy to him.

By-the-way, my dear Sir William, does it not
appear to you that versatility is the true and rare
characteristic of that rare thing called genius—
versatility and playfulness ? In my mind they are
both essential. All that is great and eminent
in past ages can boast of them—Shakespeare,
Dryden ; ay, and, when we look at *Comus* and

patronage of Queen Caroline, preferred, to a living in Suffolk.
He eventually went mad, and drowned himself in 1756 ; but
survives in an Epigram of Swift's. Mary Leapor, the most
meritorious of these three self-educated poets, is now quite
forgotten. She was the daughter of a gardener in Northampton-
shire ; who, in spite of her want of education, wrote two
volumes of very tolerable verses. She died in 1746.

L'Allegro, even our solemn Milton. As for our goodly Laureate and his fraternity, if they have them not, *tant pis pour eux* ; it will not invalidate my proposition. Whenever one of the species of animal called an authoress admires she must write verses—*c'est la règle* ; and whatever I write you are doomed to read—*c'est la règle aussi* ! So prepare yourself for a dose of bad poetry in the form of a sonnet. All sonnets are something alike ; and you will already have guessed, what I do not scruple to say in dispraise of this one, that it is as unlike Burns as possible. It is indeed the very semblance of an Italian sonnet ; so that it seems to me as if I must have composed it in Italian and then turned it into English, *concetti* and all. Now for it—

SONNET

Burns ! not the fairy songster's painted wings,
   Shaking from tiny plumes Columbian dews,
   Can match the changeful splendour of thy muse :
Now melting tenderness resistless flings
Delightful sorrow ; now quick flashing springs
   The patriot glow ; now wit the smile renews ;
   Now love with fancy blends his gayest hues,
And reason's self lies captive while he sings.
   Idol and victim of a heartless train,
Bold was thy rhyme, impetuous, sparkling, clear !
   Not Ariosto's, no, nor Shakespeare's strain
Could sooner raise or sooner quell the tear ;
   Only one tear thy magic cannot chain ;—
Burns ! Burns ! for thee it falls ! thee on thy bier !
               [Exit Admiration—enter Anger.

It is a terrible confession for a *gentle damsel* to make, that she is in a passion ; and yet so it is, and I cannot help it, and scold I must or I shall never get out of it. For you must know there are only two female resources in these cases : the best and quietest crying ; but lack-a-day and woe is me ! I never can cry except in poetry. The other is scolding, and as the offender happens to be out of my reach, you are likely to have the benefit upon paper of what I would gladly bestow upon him *viva voce*. My dear Sir William, my Marmion has won the cup at Ilsley and been cheated out of it. Think of that, my dear friend ! Won the cup upon *three legs* and been cheated out of it ! Think of that ! Won the cup upon three legs and been cheated out of it by a caricature of man—an animal as crooked in mind as in person ! Think of that, my dear friend ! Oh, that I were but a man ! Cheated by a humpback ! Think of that ! My poor Marmy, my dear Marmy, my pretty Marmy, oh, that I were but a man ! Don't you think that the monks were true sages, who refused to admit into their fraternity a member who had any cor-poreal defect ? What simpletons the Ilsley club were not to follow this excellent example ! I have known many charming deformed women, but I never knew a man of the sort good for anything in my life. Pope, for instance, what an animal was he ! Always abusing lords *en masse*, and courting them individually ; always talking like generosity and acting like avarice ; a flattery-hunter, a legacy-

hunter, a detractor, and a dupe. " He 's Knight
of the Shire, and represents them all." The only
bearable hunchback of my acquaintance is Richard
the Third. Shakespeare's Richard the Third.

Have you read Mrs. Opie's *Tales of Real Life* ?
I have only seen the first volume, and it is much
better than *Temper*. She is always powerful in
pathos. But why will she meddle with lords and
ladies ? Pray, is not your neighbour, Lady Boring-
don, an authoress ? I have heard of two novels in
high repute (but which I have not read), *Sense and
Sensibility* and *Pride and Prejudice*, ascribed to her.
The prettiest thing of the sort I have read lately
is Miss Burney's *Traits of Nature*.

Kindest compliments from all.

Ever most sincerely and affectionately yours,

MARY RUSSELL MITFORD.

To Sir William Elford, Bickham, Plymouth

BERTRAM HOUSE, *Dec.* 3, 1813.

I am sorry to say, my dear friend, that you will
have no argument on waltzing from me, and that
for a very simple reason ; namely, that I am quite
of your opinion. I cannot even imagine what the
defenders of this most *un-English* dance can find
to say for it. All that I have ever heard asserted
in its favour has been the single ejaculation, " Prejudice ! " which, when pronounced in a contemptu-
ous accent, with a becoming toss of the head, a curl
of the lip, and a proper dilatation of the nostrils,

has frequently a better effect in *dumb-founding* an adversary than all the arguments of Demosthenes or the eloquence of Cicero. This magic word, however, astounds not me. The prejudice of opinion may frequently be wrong, but the prejudice of action is commonly right ; and, right or wrong, the prejudice of modesty is always feminine.

In addition to the reasons which I suppose we have in common against this dance, I have a particular objection founded on the recollection which it always brings to my mind of a certain French dancing-master from whom I had the honour to learn it, and between whom and myself there subsisted an aversion as entire and reciprocal as ever two poor mortals were subject to. *His* reasons were pretty obvious ; then, as well as now,

> On *my stout* pegs
> Moved native awkwardness with two left legs.

My causes of dislike were, his ill-humour and his coxcombry. It was his duty to scold me into something like grace, a task which he found impossible. It was my pleasure to make him look like a fool, which was the easiest thing in the world. Very often, indeed, he saved me the trouble, and showed himself off in the most delightful way imaginable, without any pains whatever on my part. I will give you an instance.

When I was about fourteen it pleased the fates, in the shape of Miss Rowden, to inflict on her unfortunate scholars the penance of acting a play interspersed with songs, at the breaking-up time, to conclude with a grand ballet ; so that specimens might be afforded of the vast improvement of her pupils to parents, uncles, guardians, grandmammas, and second cousins.   It fell to my lot to speak the Prologue ; and at the last grand dress rehearsal, just as I was advancing from behind the scenes for that purpose, I found myself arrested by the hands of Monsieur Denis, who declared himself shocked to death at finding me placed in a situation which required me to make a curtsey, but began forthwith to make the best of a bad business by placing me in the proper station to begin this important reverence.   His design was to have a grand comprehensive *turning* curtsey, which should take in all the spectators at one sweep ; and accordingly he placed me at an angle to the right, so ╲ , where I was to begin to sink ; the sinking was to be completed straightways, so ___ ; and the rising accomplished at an equal angle to the left, so ╱ , thus describing the exact mathematical figure of a segment of a circle ⌒.   This manœuvre was repeated at least twenty times to my great annoyance ; poor Monsieur Denis scolding, fretting, and turning me about during the whole time.   At last it came to a period somewhat abruptly by the entrance of our elocution master, a sour pedant of Oxford growth, who no sooner perceived the turning curtsey than he declared it absurd, and insisted on three distinct obeisances, in the playhouse fashion. This I did not fail to interpret to Monsieur Denis,

who at last ceasing the revolution of my person
exclaimed, " *Trois révérences ! Vous ! la plus
grosse ! la plus lourde ! la plus gauche ! Trois
révérences ! Ah ! pour le coup, c'en est trop. Tenez,
monsieur,*"—but vain were his exclamations. He
had no English—our orator no French ; so at length
they fairly betook themselves to exemplifying their
respective theories in their own proper persons ;
the *maître d'éloquence* making three bobs which
were most decidedly of the neuter gender, neither
bow nor curtsey ; and the graceful Frenchman
folding his hands before him, turning on his heel
for a pivot, and making exactly the same teetotum-
like reverence that he had vainly essayed to teach
me ; both talking all the time—the Englishman in a
well-concerted harangue in his mother tongue, the
dancing-master with equal fluency letting off " legs
and wings and heads and feet " of sentences from
his untired Gallic organs. Thrice did the one
curtsey ; thrice did the other bob. But at last the
orator carried it by a triumphant majority. The
French teacher alone voted for her countryman ;
and I made three curtseys in spite of my dancing-
master.

I must not have you imagine that this, my first
and last appearance on any boards, was in any tender
tragedy or wicked comedy—anything which could
by possibility inoculate our young imaginations
with a love of the stage and its wit and its vanity.
No, my dear Sir William, our performance was one
which could never by any chance produce such an

effect ; it was neither more nor less than Miss
Hannah More's dramatic homily, *The Search after
Happiness*, and was designed equally to mend our
morals and improve our declamation.   All our
actresses, the indolent, the romantic, and the vain,
were fitted with parts which touched their respective
foibles ; as to me, *it was so difficult to discover any
fault in my charming composition* that I should
without doubt have enacted the goodly dame if I
had been a little less short, or the pattern shepherdess if I had been a little less ugly.   As it was, they
gave me the best of the worldly Misses in the shape
of—of—of Cleora (to think that I should forget my
own name !), and threw the Prologue and Epilogue
into the bargain.   I cannot say much for the moral
effect of our piece.   Just before the play began, the
lowly Maria fell into a sort of hysteric of fright,
lamentation, and anger because she was not suffered
to wear a diamond necklace which her aunt had
brought for her adornment ; and one of the
figurantes happening to overset a mug of water,
which was provided for this fit, just between
Florella and me, the gentle shepherdess gave the
poor monkey a slap on the face, and the learned
Cleora scolded most volubly in the vulgar tongue.
I cannot either say much for its historic excellence.
What between fright and bashfulness, nothing
seemed to go right ; —one muttered—another
squeaked—and a third sang all the spoken part to
a tune of her own composing.   We were regularly
too high or too low ; one did not know how to

come on—nor another how to get off. We were always out of our places, and always went the more wrong the more we tried to get right.

Divers small accidents happened, too, in this eventful evening. A little brat who acted Maria's youngest child happened to tread on part of the peel of a lemon (which had been smuggled behind the scenes by the fair Euphelia for the benefit of her voice); this peel threw the poor child on her nose, and she instantly set up a cry that made the audience laugh, and threw the actors into irretrievable confusion. Then the identical *figurante* who overthrew the water contrived to stand before the curtain at the end of the play, and I was forced to send her off before I could speak the Epilogue; to say nothing of minor ills, such as Florella's marching about with a fan instead of a nosegay—Euphelia's dropping her glove—and my dropping two lines of the Prologue, which I 'll venture to say no one missed except the prompter and the author. For the rest, our play went off exceedingly well; the few who were awake clapped at the falling of the curtain, which awoke the sleepers, and they clapped likewise.

A thousand thanks, my dear sir, for your excellent riddle. I am quite delighted with it; it is just what an enigma should be—short, graceful, and witty; and, to say everything at once—one of those rare things, a happy trifle. A German gentleman in this neighbourhood (" What has he to do with my riddle ? " Listen and you will hear)—a German

gentleman here is, you must know, a most devoted
sportsman. He has (as his wife told me about a
month ago) shot five birds in seventeen years.
Well, this gentleman was out shooting lately with a
friend and his gamekeeper, and returning home,
with plenty of game of his companion's killing but
none of his own, they happened to find a hare
sitting. " Oh," said Mr. L——, " pray let me have
one shoot at that hare, jost as she is ; I nebber have
kill one hare in my life. Pray let me have one
shoot." " It's terribly unsportsmanlike to shoot
a hare sitting ; but if you never did kill one——"
" Nebber, I assure you—except one that I thought
I did hit ; bot, as my broder fired too, I could not
be sure, and it did get away." " Well, then, fire ! "
He fired, and the hare was actually killed ! Judge,
if you can, poor Mr. L——'s ecstasy. " I do tank
you, Mr. B—— ; you are my very best friend. I
do tank you for letting me shoot this hare. I do
tank you, Mr. Gamekeeper ; I most give you one
dollar. Mr. B——, I most carry home this hare
to show to my vife, or she will not belief me."

Well, my dear sir, your riddle is positively this
nonsuch of a hare, for I never found any out in my
whole life before—except one that I discovered in
concert with a friend, who being famous for such
things claimed the whole merit of it. Now as it is
impossible that I should be so much more dull than
the dullest of the human species as never to have
found out a good riddle, I take it for granted that
all which have puzzled me were bad, and that this

" carpet " of yours is the only standard enigma
extant.   By-the-way you are yourself a very admirable solver of conundrums.   Who told you that
Hunchback was a Welshman ?   The fact really is
so, to the discredit of the Principality.   His dog
did not get the Cup, thank Heaven ! though he
cheated Marmion out of it.

Adieu, my dear sir. With the most perfect esteem,
Your obliged and affectionate friend,

M. R. M.

To Sir William Elford, Bickham

BERTRAM HOUSE, *July* 5, 1814.

MY DEAR SIR WILLIAM,

Just after my last letter I most unexpectedly went
to town, where I remained very contentedly till a
few days ago, seeing sights and hearing scandal, and
peering with shortsighted eyes to discover of what
wood crown-blocks are made.   During all this I
was, however, a little ashamed of my country, and
still more of my sex.   The frenzy was universal ;
but the ladies were as mad as maniacs at the full
of the moon—the gentlemen only in the first
quarter.   They were ladies, alas ! ladies, who
barred up Piccadilly in carriages and on foot—
ladies who hired seats at Escudier's for a guinea
an hour—ladies who rammed bank notes into the
Emperor's hand to get them consecrated by his
touch—and ladies who, to obtain a kiss of the same
magnanimous hand, threw themselves *toutes éplorées*

with nosegays at his feet. What could they have done more if it had been the Emperor Napoleon !

It is quite refreshing to turn from these barbarous Scythians with their Tartar features (I don't mean to include the King of Prussia—I admire him extremely, both in mind and person) to the *beau idéal* of royalty in Mr. Haydon's exquisite picture. I saw it to the greatest possible advantage with the mellow evening light full upon it, and not a soul in the room but our own party. Are people deserting my beautiful picture ? Perhaps I did not like it the less because you have purchased it. One thing, and one thing only, gave me pain in this charming picture ; and that is the inveterate and most distressing likeness which King Solomon bears to Queen Anne. It is Queen Anne, with beauty, with intellect, with majesty, with penetration ; but still it is Queen Anne. Did you perceive the resemblance ? It is impossible so much to admire the production without feeling a strong interest for the author—I mean the artist. Is he a man of education ; or has genius, as in Opie's case, forced itself upwards ? Is he likely to obtain employment in his own high sphere, or will he—like Sir Joshua—sink into portrait-painting ? He is your countryman, I know, as well as Sir Joshua's. I wonder, for my part, what business Devonshire has to monopolize all the men of genius !

Well, I went to see Mr. Kean, and was thoroughly disgusted. This monarch of the stage is a little

insignificant man, slightly deformed, strongly ungraceful, seldom pleasing the eye, still seldomer
satisfying the ear—with a voice between grunting
and croaking, a perpetual hoarseness which suffo-
cates his words, and a vulgarity of manner which
his admirers are pleased to call nature—the nature
of Teniers it may be, but not that of Rafaelle.   I
am quite sure that in any character where he can
possibly raise his voice above conversation pitch—
where there is anything like strong writing that he
can contrive to rant, or anything resembling passion
for him to tear to rags—his acting will always be, if
not actually insupportable, yet unequal, disappoint-
ing, and destructive of all illusion.   It is extremely
dangerous to avow this heresy.   Belles and beaux,
who know as much of the drama as my Marmion,
praise him in one word—" He electrifies me ! "
Clever men like him much, and praise him much
more, because he is not Kemble, whom I dislike
as much as they do ;   and then, for the *coup de
grâce*, up starts some elderly gentleman and knocks
you down at once with—" Madam, I have seen
Garrick, and since the days of Garrick I never
saw "—and so forth.

Do you know that Mr. Perry and I ran a very
imminent risk of standing in the pillory ourselves !
Some malicious fiend prompted me to write a libel,
and he was just going to insert it in the *Chronicle*,
when the guardian genius called Prudence, who so
seldom interferes in libel matters, interposed—
took counsel's opinion—and, to Mr. Perry's great

discontent, suppressed the epigram. I do really believe he would have ventured.

There is nothing heard of in London but Epics —ponderous *Epics*. Mr. Wordsworth has one, and Mr. Eustace is about to fatigue the world with another. To make glorious amends for all this, Mr. Moore's Persian tale is finished ; I have even seen a part of it in manuscript, and I hope in a few days to see the whole in print. He has sold it for three thousand pounds. The little I have seen is beyond all praise and all price : in these bargaining days this is not an anticlimax. God bless you, my dear friend !

Ever most affectionately yours,
M. R. MITFORD.

To Sir William Elford, Bickham

BERTRAM HOUSE, Oct. 31, 1814.

You ask me, my good friend, to recommend you some entertaining new books. Alas ! in this Gothic neighbourhood, this vile residence of Huns and Vandals, new books are as rare and almost as welcome as springs in the African deserts. Have you read Walter Scott's *Waverley* ? I have ventured to say " Walter Scott's," though I hear he denies it, just as a young girl denies the imputation of a lover ; but if there be any belief in internal evidence it must be his. It is his by a thousand indications—by all the faults and all the beauties—by the unspeakable and unrecollectable

names—by the vile pedantry of French, Latin,
Gaelic, and Italian—by the hanging the clever hero,
and marrying the stupid one—by the praise (well
deserved, certainly, for when had Scotland ever
such a friend ! but thrust in by the head and
shoulders) of the late Lord Melville—by the sweet
lyric poetry—by the perfect costume—by the
excellent keeping of the picture—by the liveliness
and gaiety of the dialogues—and last not least, by
the entire and admirable individuality of every
character in the book, high as well as low—the life
and soul which animates them all with a distinct
existence, and brings them before our eyes like the
portraits of Fielding and Cervantes.   Upon reading
this sentence over (backward, by-the-way, with the
view of finding where it began), I am struck with
the manner in which I have contrived without
story-telling to convey to you a higher idea of the
work than I entertain myself.   There is nothing
that I would unsay, and yet you would infallibly
think that I like it better than I really do ; though
I do like it very much indeed.   The character
which I prefer is the Baron of Bradwardine ; and
yet his is perhaps the least original of any ; a mere
compound—but a most entertaining compound—
of Shakespeare's Fluellen and Smollett's Lismahago.
The character that I like least is Flora McIvor,
whom the author (who ought to be the best judge)
seems to like best.   Pray tell me which are your
favourites.

If you have never read Miss Burney's *Traits of*

Nature, I would recommend that also to your perusal. It is sweetly elegant. I have not read *Mansfield Park*. *Pride and Prejudice* I thought extremely good.

I have to thank you for recommending me to a book which delights me more than almost any I ever read in my life. You of course anticipate that I must mean Walton's *Angler*. I am afraid to begin to praise it, for fear my frank should not have space enough to contain my encomiums ; but I must mention the sweet pastoral poetry, and those descriptive touches in the still sweeter and more harmonious prose, which I can compare to nothing but the tender green of the young leaves and the balmy freshness of a summer shower. The style is indescribably beautiful, and shows still the brighter for coming into immediate contact with the notes and preface of the Right Worshipful Sir John Hawkins, with his tribe of where-ofs, and where-ins, and where-bys, and with their cousins, the there-ofs, and there-ins, and there-bys, and all the vile compounds that warrants and musical dictionaries, justice-learning and fiddling-learning, could invent or produce. In point of style, all men now write pretty much alike. The good days are passed when the very arrangement of the words showed, as in Walton, in Addison, and in Johnson, almost as much as the thoughts they embodied of the writer's disposition. The diffusion of educa-tion, and partly, perhaps, the general habit of composition, has done this with your sex ; but style,

I think, though not bearing the impress of the individual in men, is still as much the criterion of mind and temper in women, as when the *Spectators* reflected, as in a mirror, the blameless purity of Addison, and the *Ramblers* showed, as in a majestic cast, the strength and sublimity of Dr. Johnson.

This is a terrible admission, for it shows that we are less cultivated ; but I do not know that it is so terrible.   Who would not rather be a Bristol farthing or a Birmingham halfpenny than one of Swift's smooth shillings ?   Now for my instances. Who can read a page of Miss Seward's writings, on any subject, without finding her out at once, from the mere putting together of the words, for the Venus and Muse of a provincial city ; the one-eyed monarch of the blind at Lichfield, who thought nobody could see elsewhere ; the pedantic coquette, and cold-hearted sensibility-monger : in a word, the female Dr. Darwin of England and literature ? Can any one open *The Countess and Gertrude* without seeing Miss Hawkins's long nose, her prejudices, her orthodoxy, in short, her worshipful papa himself in petticoats spring up before them ? Joanna Baillie's singular modesty, her noble sim-plicity, and unaffected goodness are as strongly stamped on her every sentence as her brilliant and lightsome fancy, or her commanding genius ; and the sweetness and loveliness of Mrs. Henry Tighe live in every line of her enchanting poem.

To-morrow.

Oh, my dear, dear Sir William, when you so kindly talked of my poor Marmion you never dreamed that I had been crying three days together for his loss! After distinguishing himself more than ever last year, both here and in Hampshire— after being my companion and playmate, and winding himself into my heart all the summer—in the very prime of his life, and height of his beauty, he caught the distemper, and died within a fortnight. You may well believe he did not die for want of nursing ; and so much did the care and attention I showed him, and his sweet gratitude and patience, endear him to me, that I am sure I should not have grieved half so much had he died the first day of his illness, as I did on the last. But everybody loved him. Every creature in the house cried when he died, papa inclusive—though I believe papa's grief was rather of a compound nature, a great deal for our dear Marmion, a great deal for me, and a little for the loss of the Ilsley cup.

God bless you, my dear friend ! I beg, and implore, and desire you to put yourself in a passion directly, and to write soon to your very grateful, very affectionate, and very enraged little friend,

M. R. MITFORD.

To Sir William Elford, Bickham

BERTRAM HOUSE, *Dec.* 20, 1814.

A thousand thanks to you, my dear friend, for your most kind and delightful letter. You cannot imagine how opportunely and refreshingly it came upon me. We are shut up here by the waters of this second deluge, in a sort of stationary ark—a kind of *inhabited desert island* ; and to make this misfortune the more moving, we have just lost two agreeable guests, one of whom has taken away with him all that could make such captivity supportable— papa and the greyhounds. Judge if your letter was not welcomed, like the dove and the olive branch, by those who stayed behind !

Did not you see in the newspapers a strange, romantic, and almost incredible tale of an English lady, with a little daughter, a female friend, and a maid-servant, who were taken in a Swedish vessel bound from Lisbon to Bordeaux, by a Barbary corsair—carried to Algiers—neither suffered to land or to refit—turned adrift without provisions— becalmed for seven days on their way to Gibraltar— and finally put under quarantine at that place for six weeks, before they were permitted to proceed to their original destination ? That lady was Mrs. Perry.[1] Think, my dear friend, what must have been her personal sufferings and her mental

[1] Wife of Mr. Perry of the *Morning Chronicle*, and mother of Sir Erskine Perry.

anguish ; think of the mother's agony and the
woman's fears ; and admire with me the fortitude
which enabled her already-debilitated constitution
to struggle through such complicated evils ! She
survived them ; but she will not, I fear, survive
them long. Every account is worse and worse. A
shower, a mist, a blast of air, even the passage of a
cloud over the sun, is to her a new disease ; and
soon, very soon, will this invaluable woman, in
whom all the virtues are adorned by all the graces,
be lost to those who love her as a wife, a mother, and
a friend. What beauty, what talent, what goodness
will die with her ! The leading character of her
mind and person was, indeed, a majestic purity, a
dignified simplicity, a propriety almost intuitive, of
which the polish was so intense that it almost
repelled. I have never seen a woman who would
have been so entirely feared had she not been
entirely loved. But under that composed exterior,
what sensibility, what wit, what warmth of heart
disclosed itself to her friends ! And of all those
friends, who will lament her as I shall ! for to
whom—all kindness as she is—has she ever been
so kind ! My mother only could be dearer or more
respected.

But I meant, my dear Sir William, to write you a
gay letter, and behold I have suffered this melan-
choly subject to seize on my pen, and I shall
presently make you as vapourish as myself.

To change the subject, I must give you an anecdote which impressed me much, connected with

the late horrible affair of Sir Henry Mildmay and
Lady Rosebery. My authority is a letter from
Mr. Poulet Mildmay to a gentleman in Winchester.
Sir Henry Mildmay, on his return from Scotland
to his London house with the partner of his guilt,
said to his housekeeper, " You know Lady Rosebery
—she wishes you to continue with us—you must
go directly to Winchester and get St. John's House
ready for our reception." " Am I, sir," asked this
firm and virtuous domestic—" am I to prepare for
her ladyship the apartment in which her sister
died ? " It is scarcely necessary to add that the
guilty pair did not take Winchester in their road to
the continent.

Did I, when talking of *Waverley*, tell you that I
had happened a year or two ago to meet with a most
curious book—alluded to, though not named, in
that work—entitled, *Some Passages in the Life of
Colonel Gardiner*, by Dr. Doddridge ? This Colonel
Gardiner is the Colonel G—— of *Waverley*, and
this biographical *morceau* is exactly calculated to
form *le pendant* to the life of Johanna Southcote
with which Mr. Toser will probably some day
favour the world. The supernatural illumination
is precisely the same in both cases, though I cannot
find that the worthy colonel ever fancied himself
in the family-way, or that he ever made any money
of his conversion. Of course he was more fool
and she is more knave—if knave can ever be feminine, which, alas ! for the sex, I fear it can.

I am still firmly of opinion that Walter Scott had

some share in *Waverley* ; and I know not the
evidence that should induce me to believe that
Dugald Stewart had anything to do with it.   He !
the triptologist !—as Horace Walpole says.   He !
the style-monger, whose periods, with their nice
balancing and their elaborate finish, always remind
me of a worthy personage in blue and silver, yclept,
I believe, the Flemish Hercules, whom I have seen
balancing a ladder on his finger, with three children
on one end and two on the other—he write that
half French, half English, half Scotch, half Gaelic,
half Latin, half Italian—that hotch-potch of
languages—that movable Babel called *Waverley* !
My dear Sir William, there is not in the whole
book one single page of pure and vernacular English;
there is not one single period, of which you forget
the sense in admiration of the sound.

The want of elegance is almost the only want in
Miss Austen.   I have not read her *Mansfield Park* ;
but it is impossible not to feel in every line of *Pride
and Prejudice*, in every word of Elizabeth, the entire
want of taste which could produce so pert, so worldly
a heroine as the beloved of such a man as Darcy.
Wickham is equally bad.   Oh ! they were just fit
for each other, and I cannot forgive that delightful Darcy for parting them.   Darcy should have
married Jane.   He is of all the admirable characters
the best designed and the best sustained.   I quite
agree with you in preferring Miss Austen to Miss
Edgeworth.   If the former had a little more taste,
a little more perception of the graceful, as well as of

the humorous, I know not indeed any one to whom I
should not prefer her.   There is none of the hard-
ness, the cold selfishness, of Miss Edgeworth about
her writings ; she is in a much better humour with
the world ; she preaches no sermons ; she wants
nothing but the *beau idéal* of the female character
to be a perfect novel-writer ; and perhaps even
that *beau idéal* would only be missed by such a
petite maîtresse in books as myself, who would never
admit a muse into my library till she had been
taught to dance by the Graces.

I am much obliged to you, my dear friend, for
your kind condolence on the death of poor Marmion.
I have appointed a successor to his post of pet greyhound in the shape of a beautiful black puppy
called Moss Trooper, who is already as large as a
good-sized donkey, and incomparably glossy and
graceful.   I am sadly afraid of losing him ; I am
so unfortunate in my favourites—but as he is only
fifteen months old, has had the distemper, has a
glorious appetite, and promises faithfully never to
die as long as he lives, I have great hopes of him.
He begs his compliments to Tray, *though unknown*,
and I beg mine to Tray's fair mistress.

Ever, my dear sir,
Most sincerely and affectionately yours,
M. R. Mitford.

P.S.—What is become of the " History of the
Waltz " which I so much wish to see ?

I have, since this was written, been reading both

the false and the true letters on France and Ireland
of Mr. Curran, which have made so much noise in
the world ; and, odd as it may seem, I think the
letter which Mr. Curran so stoutly denies much
more like his other writings, more distinguished by
his peculiar style, than the one he avows ! The
former is full of wild fancy and bitter wit—clear,
nervous, and (to say all in one word) completely
Irish, both in its faults and beauties ; the latter,
with some tolerable passages, is in the main turgid,
bombastic, full of an unintelligible *muddy depth*—
of feelings terribly refined, and distinctions without
a difference—in a word, completely German.
Madame De Staël alone could rival him in the art
of making nonsense look like sense.   Did you ever
meet Mr. Curran ?   His conversation is said to be
unrivalled.

He was once staying in company with Godwin
at the house of a friend of mine.   Mr. Godwin, as
usual, pretended to go to sleep after dinner.   That
it was only make-believe was, however, very visible ;
and Curran seized the opportunity to treat his
worthy host with a character of Godwin the most
bitter that his wit and his malice could invent,
qualifying every phrase with " though he is my
friend."   The contortions of the philosopher, who
dared not show he was awake during this castiga-
tion, and the pretended fear which Curran showed
of awakening him ; the concealed anger of the one
when he did venture to open his eyes, and the
assumed innocence of the other ; formed a scene

which no comedy ever equalled. The advocate of sincerity, the frank philosopher Godwin, has, however, never forgiven this exemplification of his theory. God bless you ! Adieu.

To Sir William Elford, Bickham

BERTRAM HOUSE, *Feb.* 13, 1815.

Are you, my dear friend, of the Wordsworth school ?   I think not ; so I may venture to say that I do not much like that either.   There is such a waste of talent—such imagination buried alive—in that vast wordy wilderness ; such powers lavished upon a pedlar ; such poetry thrown away on dull metaphysics—that antidote to poetry.   Who is it says that " when one man is talking to another who does not understand him, and when he that is talking does not understand himself, that is meta-physics " ?   I never did like dreams and visions and allegories, even in Addison and Spencer.   À *propos* to painting, what is your *protégé* Mr. Haydon about ?   Are we to have *le pendant* to the " Judg-ment of Solomon " in the next Exhibition ?   I hope Mr. Haydon will not desert the Old Testament. It appears to me that the great Italian painters have almost exhausted the New ; and I even think that there is more of variety, of splendour, of human feeling and passion in the Old, than in that pure and holy and godlike life, whose tears were tears of pity, and whose power was to save.   You will not mis-understand me when I say that the ardent and erring

David is a better hero for painting.   God bless you,
my dear friend !   Pray write soon to
      Your sincere and affectionate admirer,
                MARY RUSSELL MITFORD.

To Sir William Elford, Bickham, Plymouth

BERTRAM HOUSE, *April* 3, 1815.

Alas ! my dear friend, you are mistaken—quite
mistaken, I assure you.   I am not going to be
married.   No such good luck, as papa says.   I
have not been courted, and I am not in love.   So
much for this question.   If I ever should happen
to be going to be married (elegant construction
this!) I will then not fail to let you into the secret ;
but alas ! alas ! alas !   " In such a *then* I write a
never."

  Pray have you read *The Lord of the Isles* ?
I do not mean, as I once unwittingly did in the
beginning of our correspondence, to draw you into
the scrape of reading a poem ; but, if you should
by chance have looked at it, pray tell me how you
like it.   It is certainly a thousand times better than
Rokeby, and yet it does not please me as Scott's
poems used to do.   I am afraid that I once admired
him a great deal too much ; and now am in some
danger of liking him a great deal too little.   Nothing
is so violent as a rebound, either of the head or the
heart.   Once extinguished, enthusiasm and all the
fire in Vesuvius will never light it again.   I fancy
that the world is something of my mind in this

respect, and begins to tire of its idol. Only the world is not half so honest, and instead of knocking down one piece of wood, contents itself with sticking up another right before it. " It is not," say all the gentle damsels of my acquaintance, " that we like Scott less—we only like Lord Byron better." Now I do not—I like Scott less—but Lord Byron less still. The only *modern* poet whom I like better and better is Campbell.

I have told you that I would not put you in danger of being jingled into a fever by " mincing poesy " ; but I have found out, to my great satisfaction, that I shan't affront you by recommending a prose epic to your perusal ; and I have lately been very much and very unexpectedly pleased with Lady Morgan's (*ci-devant* Miss Owensen) *O'Donnel*. I had a great prejudice and dislike to this fair authoress ever since I read a certain description of which she was guilty, where part of a lady's dress is described as " an apparent tissue of woven air," and really took up the book with an idea that nothing but nonsense could come from that quarter. I was, however, very much disappointed in my malicious expectations of laughing at her, and obliged to content myself with laughing with her. Her hero is very interesting—her heroine very amusing. There are some good characters, particularly a managing bustling woman of fashion ; *et pour la bonne bouche* there is an Irish servant not much, if at all, inferior to the admirable Irishmen of Miss Edgeworth.

À propos to novels, I have discovered that our
great favourite, Miss Austen, is my countrywoman ;
that mamma knew all her family very intimately ;
and that she herself is an old maid (I beg her pardon
—I mean a young lady) with whom mamma before
her marriage was acquainted. Mamma says that
she was then the prettiest, silliest, most affected,
husband-hunting butterfly she ever remembers ;
and a friend of mine, who visits her now, says that
she has stiffened into the most perpendicular, precise, taciturn piece of " single blessedness " that
ever existed, and that, till *Pride and Prejudice*
showed what a precious gem was hidden in that
unbending case, she was no more regarded in
society than a poker or a fire-screen, or any other
thin upright piece of wood or iron that fills its corner
in peace and quietness. The case is very different
now ; she is still a poker—but a poker of whom
every one is afraid. It must be confessed that this
silent observation from such an observer is rather
formidable. Most writers are good - humoured
chatterers—neither very wise nor very witty :—
but nine times out of ten (at least in the few that I
have known) unaffected and pleasant, and quite
removing by their conversation any awe that may
have been excited by their works. But a wit, a
delineator of character, who does not talk, is terrific
indeed !

After all, I do not know that I can quite vouch for
this account, though the friend from whom I
received it is truth itself ; but her family connec-

tions must render her disagreeable to Miss Austen, since she is the sister-in-law of a gentleman who is at law with Miss A.'s brother for the greater part of his fortune. You must have remarked how much her stories hinge upon entailed estates ; doubtless she has learnt to dislike entails. Her brother was adopted by a Mr. Knight, who left him his name and two much better legacies in an estate of five thousand a year in Kent, and another of nearly double the value in Hampshire ; but it seems he forgot some ceremony—passing a fine, I think they call it—with regard to the Hampshire property, which Mr. Baverstock has claimed in right of his mother, together with the mesne rents, and is likely to be successful. Before I quite drop the subject of novels, I must tell you that I am reading *Guy Mannering* with great pleasure. I have not finished it nearly, so that I speak of it now as any one would do that had read no further than the second volume of the *Mysteries of Udolpho*, and that would be much better than one who had finished it. I do not think that Walter Scott did write *Guy Mannering* ; it is not nearly so like him as *Waverley* was, and the motto is from *The Lay*.

I am quite happy that you are of my opinion with regard to Scripture heroes ; I always think myself so safe when you agree with me. It was, however, natural in Mr. Haydon to wish to draw the bow of Ulysses and try the subject which has engaged all the great masters. Mr. Eustace, I think it is, who has objected to the exaggerated expression of meekness which distinguishes the Christ of the Italian painters. In those which I have seen I should rather complain of the *entire absence* of the expression of power—power latent, dormant, in repose, but still power—still that power which could without exertion, with unaltered calmness, heal the sick and raise the dead. It would be less absurd to paint a sleeping Hercules without the appearance of strength, than to delineate our Saviour without the expression of power. No one can so well supply this defect as Mr. Haydon, and he is very likely to have done it.

Always most affectionately yours,

M. R. M.

To Sir William Elford, Bickham

BERTRAM HOUSE, *May* 13, 1815.

Oh, my dear Sir William, what a sad flatterer you are ! I blushed from my eyes to my fingers' ends, neck, ears, and elbows included—blushed like—like—do help me to a simile—blushed like beetroot, on reading your dear, charming, fibbing letter. But I am sadly afraid that I smiled too, and that the flattery was a great deal more welcome than, as the wise are wont to say, flattery ever ought to be. . . .

With regard to novels, I should like to see one undertaken without any plot at all. I do not mean that it should have no story ; but I should like some writer of luxuriant fancy to begin with a certain set

of characters—one family, for instance—without
any preconceived design further than one or two
incidents and dialogues, which would naturally
suggest fresh matter, and so proceed in this way,
throwing in incidents and characters profusely, but
avoiding all stage tricks and strong situations, till
some death or marriage should afford a natural
conclusion to the book. Is this quite impossible ?
I think not. Our grandmothers, when about to
make a *beau pot*, proceeded, I fancy, much as their
gardeners when clipping a yew hedge or laying
out a parterre. Every stalk and stem was in its
place ; tulip answered tulip, and peony stared at
peony. Even a rebellious leaf was reduced to order,
and the huge bouquet spread its tremendous width
as flat, as stiff, and almost as ugly as its fair framer's
painted fan. We, their granddaughters, throw our
honeysuckles and roses into their vases with little
other care than to produce the grace of nature by
its carelessness and profusion. And why should
we not do so by the flowers of fancy ?

The only thing that I cannot forgive in Mrs.
Carter is the most unaccountable contempt with
which she talks of the *Odyssey*, the sweetest specimen of Grecian genius, and a picture of ancient
manners so perfect because so undesigned. Every
one who reads the descriptions of Gothic costume
in Walter Scott, and of Turkish habits in Lord
Byron, must be convinced by their very elaborate-
ness and detail that they tell of things new both
to them and their readers—things of which they

know but little.   All their panoply of love or war,
their Turkish boudoirs and their Gothic drinking-
halls, cups, amulets, rosaries, mazers and all, are
set down as part of the fiction ; and we never find
out that so it might have been, till some good old
gentleman is kind enough to tell us so in a note.
But every touch of costume, every minute stroke
of manners in Homer, comes on us at once with the
clearness, the freshness, and the loveliness of truth.
I speak of this, perhaps, with the more enthusiasm
because I have lately been reading Dr. Clarke's
Travels in the Troas, with an interest which would
almost appear ricidulous in one who has only read
Homer in her mother tongue ; but I always
worshipped his genius as second only to our
own Shakespeare's, and always loved the *Odyssey*
best.

Among the thousand and one instances of kindness and indulgence that I owe to you, my own dear
friend, I do not know any one which more deserves
my thanks than your unheard-of forbearance in
abstaining from crowing over me on the score of
my poor friend, Lord Cochrane, who is certainly,
to say the least of the matter, a little straitwaistcoat-
ish.   Do not, however, because I acknowledge him
to be a little mad, understand me to admit that he
is guilty ; but mad he most undoubtedly must be
—his escape and his return both prove it.   He was
always a man of reverie, of deep musings, of
concentrated imagination.   The things that passed
before his bodily eye made little impression on

his mind.   He lived rather to fancy and the future,
than to the present and the real.

Affectionately yours,

M. R. M.

To Sir William Elford, Bickham, Plymouth

BERTRAM HOUSE, *August* 20, 1815.

What shall I talk to you about, my dear friend ?
Shall I tell you that our beaux are all in despair
because we had no races this year, and most un-
gallantly revenged their cause on the unfortunate
belles by not attending the ball, by courtesy called
a Peace Ball, and leaving the aforesaid belles to
dance by themselves, so that the despair was
universal ; extending, I verily believe, to every
damsel in the neighbourhood except your poor
little friend, who has no great love of races, and
something very like an aversion to balls ?

What, indeed, should I do at a dance with my
dumpling of a person tumbling about like a cricket-
ball on uneven ground, or a bowl rolling among
nine-pins—casting off with the grace of a frisky
Yorkshire cow, or going down the middle with
the majesty of an overloaded hay-waggon passing
through a narrow lane ?   What should I do at a
ball ?   I have not been at one for these two years,
and never, if I can avoid it, mean to go to one again.
The present passion of the neighbourhood, indeed
—of the male part of it, I mean—is not dancing
but cricket.   I have a great admiration for this

manly exercise, which really engrosses all the souls and bodies of all the men, high and low, within twenty miles of this place. My love of it arises, I suppose, from the influence of local attachment, as your countryman, Mr. Polwhele, would call it. Alresford is or will be celebrated in history for two things ; the first—to speak modestly—is my birth ; the second is cricket. Cricket is to Alresford what beer is to Dorchester, or cakes to Shrewsbury. Hampshire is the Greece of cricketers, and Alresford the Athens. Papa, too, has a great fondness for this truly English sport, and " though he plays no more, o'erlooks the *balls*."

Pray tell me if you are a cricketer. I have a great notion that you are, but my father says you have not in all your country level space enough for a cricket-ground : I have a prodigious idea that this is a fib. Gratify, I beseech you, my dutiful inclination by telling me that it is.

God bless you, my dear Sir William ! Papa and mamma join in kindest regards and good wishes.

Ever most affectionately yours,

MARY RUSSELL MITFORD.

To Sir William Elford, Bickham, Plymouth

BERTRAM HOUSE, *Sept.* 18, 1815.

I was very much entertained with your admirable Quaker story ; but I still can't help having a sneaking kindness for the sect ; not perhaps for its religious tenets, but for its peaceableness, its

industry, its simplicity, and its frankness. I do
not dislike their singularity either. In our present
high state of civilisation, people are so much alike,
that anything at all odd comes on one with the
freshness and character of an antique coin among
smooth shillings. I must confess, however, that I
do not know many Quakers, which may be one
reason of my partiality ; since of the few I have
met with, the men have been shrewd and honest,
and the women have had minds as fair, as pure, and
as delicate as their dove-eyed beauty or their spotless dress. This terrible anticlimax warns me to
go to bed. It smells of drowsiness, does it not ?
It fairly nods, and I dare say you are nodding too.
Good-night, good-night, and God bless you ! and
believe me ever, sleeping or waking,

> Most affectionately yours,
> M. R. MITFORD.

To Sir William Elford, Bickham, Plymouth

BERTRAM HOUSE, *Oct.* 20, 1816.

It has always been to me a very sufficient reason
for not liking *Hamlet*, that it is the chosen and
favourite play of all those German metaphysicians,
Schlegel, Goethe, Madame De Staël, and Co.—
persons who, while they are thoroughly incapable
of appreciating the greater and more obvious
beauties of our immortal poet, make him contribute
to their own little vanity, by seizing hold of some

equivocal passage, crying it up as a gem of their own finding, and talking " about it, goddess, and about it." My favourite play (" tell it not in Gath ! ") is the first part of *King Henry the Fourth*. All the whining, crying, canting heroes that ever lived have less hold upon my affections—less power of interesting me—of carrying me off my legs (as a lady said of Burns), than that most delightful and most natural creature, the " Gunpowder Percy," the " Hotspur of the North." I am always a rebel when I see that play, and could never be reconciled to the catastrophe, were not Falstaff on the other side. Pray do you believe that Falstaff was a coward, a liar, a flatterer, and a glutton ? Are you not sure that all this is calumny, and that the humorous knight was a most valiant and gentle-manly, as well as a most delightful person ? I am quite convinced of it, and cannot forgive Henry the Fifth for his shabby treatment of him after his father's death.

Next to this I like *The Merry Wives of Windsor*, *Romeo and Juliet*, *Macbeth*, *The Tempest*, *The Midsummer Night's Dream*, *Richard the Third*, *As You Like It*, and last, not least, *Much Ado About Nothing*. The Beatrice of this last play is indeed my standard of female wit and almost of female character ; nothing so lively, so clever, so un-affected, and so warmhearted, ever trod this work-a-day world. Benedick is not quite equal to her ; but this in female eyes is no great sin. Shakespeare saw through nature, and knew which

sex to make the cleverest. There's a challenge for
you ! Will you take up the glove ?

You will find from this poetical confession of faith
that I have a strong preference to comedy, and the
fact, ignoble as it is, must be avowed. I even go so
far as to think his comedies, and those parts of his
tragedies which resemble comedy, the great and
unrivalled distinction of Shakespeare. Many of
his immediate successors approach him very nearly
in tragic powers ; Massinger equals him in declamation ; Ford in sublimity ; Fletcher in pathos :
but no one comes near him in wit. Ben Jonson's
best play is at a thousand leagues' distance.

I have at last safely disposed of my bride, to my
infinite comfort and relief. Very grand wedding !
Plenty of barouches and bridesmaids, cake and
favours, kissing and crying ! The bride, indeed,
had amused herself with the last-mentioned recreation for a whole week, and having, moreover,
accumulated on her person so much finery in the
shape of lace flounces, spensers, bonnets, veils, and
scarfs that she looked as if by mistake she had put
on two wedding-dresses instead of one, was by
many degrees the greatest fright I ever saw in my
life. Indeed, between crying and blushing, brides,
and bridesmaids too, do generally look strange
figures : I am sure we did—though, to confess the
truth, I really could not cry, much as I wished to
keep all my neighbours in countenance, and was
forced to hold my handkerchief to my eyes and sigh
in vain for " *ce don de dames que Dieu ne m'a pas*

donné." I don't really think if I were married myself I should have the grace to shed a tear. For the rest, all went off extremely well, except two small accidents, one of which discomposed me very much. One of my fellow-bridesmaids put on her skirt wrong-side outwards, and though half a dozen abigails offered to *transplant* the lace and bows from one side to the other, and though I all but went down on my knees to beg her not to turn it, turn it she would, and turn it she did—the obstinate ! The other mischance was our entirely forgetting to draw any cake through the ring, so that our fate still rests in abeyance.

The bride and her second sister set off to Brighton, and I and the youngest remained to do the honours of the wedding-dinner. Of course we all got tipsy —those who were used to it comfortably enough, and those who were not, rather awkwardly—some were top-heavy and wanted tying up like overblown carnations, some reeled, some staggered—and one fell, and catching at a harp for a prop, came down with his supporter and a salver of coffee which he knocked out of the servant's hands ; such a crash, vocal and instrumental, I never heard in my life !

To Sir William Elford, Bickham, Plymouth

BERTRAM HOUSE, *Nov.* 24, 1816.

I was greatly shocked last week, my dear Sir William, by the sudden death of a most kind and worthy friend, Mr. Newell of Whitby Park, near

Reading. He made a coursing party for me on
Thursday, and on Sunday he was in his coffin.
Active, cheerful, hospitable, intelligent, he was one
of the most respectable of that respectable class,
the great English farmer. I never, indeed, knew
any one so thoroughly English, in person, manner,
and mind. Firm, stout, and upright as one of his
own oaks, he had a countenance combining a great
deal of weatherbeaten middle-aged beauty with a
look of irresistible kindness, frankness, and good-
humour—a voice that might have hailed a ship at
sea without the assistance of a speaking-trumpet—
and a heart that trusted to that voice every movement of its honest and generous feelings. He is a
man who must be lamented by all who knew him ;
and his particular attention and constant kindness
to me add to my loss and my regret. But every
one dies who is kind to me. Take care of yourself,
my dear Sir William. *En attendant*, God bless you !
      Most sincerely and affectionately yours,
                    MARY RUSSELL MITFORD.

      To Sir William Elford, Bickham, Plymouth

                    BERTRAM HOUSE, *Dec.* 23, 1816.

MY DEAR FRIEND,

    I am very glad that we agree so well respecting
the *Antiquary* and Meg Merrilies. She certainly is
a very melodramatic personage ; and the admiration she excites is a proof of the same vitiated taste
which leads to the preference of pieces of mere

spectacle to the legitimate drama. Besides her pretensions to prophecy, Colonel Mannering is, as you observe, correct in his " nativities." Do you know that this book has brought astrology into some degree of repute again ? An instance of this has actually occurred in my own knowledge. A young Oxfordshire lady, of a character exactly resembling Miss Austen's " Harriet Smith," with the same prettiness, the same good-humour, the same simplicity, and the same knack of falling into love, and out of love, and into love again, had a scheme of life erected about two months ago. The conjuror took care to tell her several things which had happened in her family, and were well known to all the neighbourhood—many things, too, he told her of lovers and offers—much of husbands and children ; but as the last and most solemn warning he told her to beware of fire in her thirtieth year. She heard it with horror—a horror that shocked and alarmed the whole family. It was some time before she could be prevailed upon to reveal the cause, and when discovered she took to her bed for a fortnight. Ought not this man to be punished ?

I am just now reading a very different book, one of which I had before read an abridgment, and indeed some part of the original, but not the whole —Bruce's *Travels in Abyssinia*. Did you ever read them ? No words can express the pleasure they have given me. I was never, I think, so carried away by a man in my life. Such courage, such

fortitude, such power of mind and body ;—there
is the grand charm after all—it is the *command* of
genius that carries a woman off her feet ! The
singular mixture of romantic adventure and historical truth—the strange fate of the book, too,
cried down for so many years as a series of false-
hoods, and then proved by Dr. Clark and Mr. Salt,
and half a dozen other travellers to be true, even in
its most improbable details ! For my part, I cannot
conceive how the accusation of falsehood, though it
might affect its credit, could diminish its sale (it
once, they say, might be bought as waste paper),
since to me it would as a work of genius have been
equally delightful, and perhaps still more wonderful
as an invention than as a reality.

Nobody finds fault with Defoe's *Robinson Crusoe*,
or that more extraordinary deception of his, the
Journal of the Great Plague of London, because they
are works of imagination ; and I do not understand
why Mr. Bruce's adventures might not have been
allowed the same licence. I can, however, quite
understand the delightful haughtiness which induced him to refuse answering any questions, and
to tell his questioners to go and see. I quite
understand that part of his character. It is just as
Milton would have said ; just as Burns. Oh, he
was a hero of the right stamp ! and I am really quite
sorry that everybody should believe and admire him
now ; that I might not have the pleasure of believ-
ing and admiring him all to myself. In the mean
time I do my best to do him honour. I have had

a present of bantams, who are great pets and great beauties, and I have christened them all after Mr. Bruce's Abyssinian friends. My cock, an astonishingly lovely golden creature, is the old Ras Michael—his favourite wife is Ozoro Esther, and the other lady is Tecla Mariam. I must confess that I have not yet quite vanquished the difficulties of this nomenclature. My pets themselves do not (except when I have the barley measure in my hand) answer to it so readily as to Biddy, Biddy !

Are you not astonished at Dr. Parr's marriage ? though I am not sure if it has taken place yet. But he has actually found a lady of fifty, with a good fortune, willing to take him " for better, for worse," and is to be joined to her forthwith. Do you happen to know this *savant*, with his wig and his pipe ? I do not know that I was ever so much disappointed in any one. I expected a Dr. Johnson —large, and tall, and loud, and stately—and then to see a little strange figure, and hear such a lisping, mumbling voice ! It was falling from Alexander the Great to Tom Thumb the Little.

Adieu, my dear friend. Papa and mamma join in kindest remembrance. And I am ever

Most affectionately yours,

M. R. MITFORD.

To Sir William Elford, Bickham, Plymouth

BERTRAM HOUSE, *Sept.* 13, 1817.

Yes, my dear friend, this fine weather has been quite a renewal of the feelings and beauty of the early summer ; for the precious rains have pre-served all the verdure, and we have now a second June, with its bright skies, its green hedgerows, its haymakings, and its woodbines. I cannot tell you how thoroughly I enjoy it. I should, however, certainly enjoy it much more were I not very honestly and conscientiously trying to like riding on horseback—a detestable recreation, which I abhor the more the more I endeavour to endure it. The exercise, which I do dearly love, is to be whirled along fast, fast, fast, by a blood horse in a gig ; this, under a bright sun, with a brisk wind full in my face, is my highest notion of physical pleasure; even walking is not so exhilarating. Besides this experiment upon my bodily taste, I have been making one of the same nature on my mind— trying to learn to admire Wordsworth's poetry. I do not mean by " admire " merely to like and applaud those fine passages which all the world must like, but to admire *en masse*—all, every page, every line, every word, every comma ; to admire nothing else, and to admire all day long. This is what Mr. Wordsworth expects of his admirers (I had almost said his worshippers) ; and, strange to say, a large proportion of the cleverest young men in London (your friend Mr. Haydon among the rest) do pay him this homage.

One of the circle, a Reading gentleman of the name of Talfourd—of whom, by the way, when he has completed his studies for the bar, the world will one day hear a good deal—talked to me about Mr. Wordsworth's genius till I began to be a little ashamed of not admiring him myself. Enthusiasm is very catching, especially when it is very eloquent. So I set about admiring. To be sure, there was the small difficulty of not understanding ; but that, as Mr. Talfourd said, did not signify. So I admired. But, alas ! my admiration was but a puny, flickering flame, that wanted constant re-lighting at Mr. Talfourd's enthusiasm, and constant fanning by Mr. Talfourd's eloquence. He went to town, and out it went for good. After all, I should never have done for a disciple of Mr. Wordsworth. I have too much self-will about me—too much spirit of opposition. By-the-by, I wonder how Mr. Haydon manages. Docility is not *his* characteristic. I suppose there is a little commerce of flattery, though Mr. Wordsworth not only exacts an entire relinquishment of all other tastes besides taste for his poetry, but if an unlucky votary chances to say, " Of all your beautiful passages I most admire so and so," he knocks him down by saying, " Sir, I have a thousand passages more beautiful than that. Sir, you know nothing of the matter." One's conscience may be pretty well absolved for not admiring this man : he admires himself enough for all the world put together.

The best estimate I ever met with of Wordsworth's powers is in Coleridge's very out-of-the-way, but very amusing *Biographia Literaria*. It is in the highest degree flattering, but it admits that he may have faults ; and Mr. Lamb, who knows them both well, says he is sure Mr. Wordsworth will never speak to Mr. Coleridge again. Have you met with the *Biographia Literaria* ? It has, to be sure, rather more absurdities than ever were collected together in a printed book before ; but there are passages written with sunbeams. The pleasantry throughout is as ungraceful as a dancing cow, and every page gives you reason to suspect that the author had forgotten the page that preceded it. I have lately heard a curious anecdote of Mr. Coleridge, which, at the risk—at the certainty—of spoiling it in the telling, I cannot forbear sending you. He had for some time relinquished his English mode of intoxication by brandy and water for the Turkish fashion of intoxication by opium ; but at length the earnest remonstrances of his friends, aided by his own sense of right, prevailed on him to attempt to conquer this destructive habit. He put himself under watch and ward ; went to lodge at an apothecary's at Highgate, whom he cautioned to lock up his opiates ; gave his money to a friend to keep ; and desired his druggist not to trust him. For some days all went on well. Our poet was ready to hang himself ; could not write, could not eat, could not—incredible as it may seem—could not talk. The stimulus was wanting, and the apothecary contented. Suddenly, however, he began to mend ; he wrote, he read, he talked, he harangued ; Coleridge was himself again ! And the apothecary began to watch within doors and without. The next day the culprit was detected ; for the next day came a second supply of laudanum from Murray's, well wrapped up in proof sheets of the *Quarterly Review*.

Before leaving the subject of books, I must ask you if you have read *Lalla Rookh* ? If I ever ventured to recommend poetry to you, I think I should say, do read that. But I dare not run the risk. I will, however, caution you, if you *should* take it up, against judging it by the first story, which is quite Lord Byron-ish in plan and metre, and would have been equally detestable in sentiment and execution, but that the " Spirit of Love, Spirit of bliss " would force itself through. No thanks to the author that it is not as hating and disagreeable as " Lara " or " Manfred." I am quite convinced that he would have made it so if he could. The tale by which I would have you judge of Moore is the last, " The Light of the Harem "—the sweetest, the lightest, the most elegant trifle ever written by man. Pray do read this—it is not above fifty pages.

We are likely to have the Duke of Wellington for a neighbour here at Lord Rivers's place, provided he should himself approve the situation, which I

cannot but doubt.   Strathfieldsaye is a pretty rural
place enough, with a great deal of swampy-looking
water, very little inequality of ground, and a belt of
firs all round.   Altogether it gives the idea and the
feeling of water meadows, with a few fine trees
scattered about, and on a hot day looks cool and
pleasant ; but there is nothing about it of the grand
and commanding, nor even of the picturesque ; nor
do I think that the united powers of the architect
and the landscape gardener could ever convert it
into such a scene as ought to encircle a national
palace.   The great recommendation is, the value
of the surrounding property and the extent of
manorial rights.   I shall be sorry to lose the
greyhounds.

Ever, my dear Sir William,

Your affectionate friend,

M. R. MITFORD.

I had not heard of Miss Austen's death.   What
a terrible loss !   Are you quite sure that it is our
Miss Austen ?

To Sir William Elford, Bickham

BERTRAM HOUSE, *August*, 1818.

Did I ever give you a sketch of that excellent
but very singular personage Dr. Valpy ?   He is to
Dr. Parr what Dr. Parr is to Dr. Johnson—the copy
of a copy, the shadow of a shade ; very learned,
very dictatorial, very knock-me-down ; vainer than
a peacock, or Dr. Parr, or than both of them put

together. He is indeed the abstract idea of a
schoolmaster embodied ; you may know his profession a mile off. Well, he is going to have a
Greek play performed by the boys ; the Hercules
—Hercules—Hercules something—I cannot remember ; but I believe it is the Greek for mad,
and it is to be followed by an English play for the
ladies and the country gentlemen, and this English
play is, what do you think ? The second part of
Henry the Fourth, leaving out Falstaff and Justice
Shallow ! My dear Sir William, is not this good
man essentially mad ? I fairly scolded. Flesh and
blood could not bear it. Ever, my dear friend,

Most affectionately yours,

M. R. MITFORD.

To Sir William Elford, *Post Office*, *Bath*

BERTRAM HOUSE, *Nov*. 9, 1818.

Yes, my dear Sir William, your prognostics were
right ; a scolding letter was actually written and
sent off two days before I received the charming
packet about which you are pleased to talk so much
nonsense in the way of apology. You must forgive
the scolding, and you will forgive it, I am sure ; for
you know I was not then apprised of the grand evils
of mind and body by which you were assailed—the
teeth and the rats. I hope those enemies are in a
good train to be overcome and cured—that the
teeth are multiplying and the rats decreasing.
N.B.—If you want a first-rate breed of cats we can

supply you. We have a white cat, half Persian, as deaf as a post, with one eye blue and the other yellow, who, besides being a great beauty, is the best rat-catcher in the county. Shall we save you one of the next litter of white kittens ?

You ask me about Blackwood's *Edinburgh Magazine* : I will tell you just what it is—a very libellous, naughty, wicked, scandalous, story-telling, entertaining work—a sort of chapel-of-ease to my old friend, the *Quarterly Review* ; abusing all the wits and poets and politicians of *our* side, and praising all of *yours* ; abusing Hazlitt, abusing John Keats, abusing Leigh Hunt, abusing (and that is really too bad) abusing Haydon, and lauding Mr. Gifford, Mr. Croker, and Mr. Canning. But all this, especially the abuse, is very cleverly done ; and I think you would be amused by it. I particularly recommend to you the poetical notices to correspondents, the " Mad Banker of Amsterdam," and some letters on the sagacity of the shepherd's dog, by that delightful poet James Hogg.

Were you not heart-struck at the awful catastrophe of Sir Samuel Romilly ? The sacrifice of his own reputation, the very victim of admiration and respect ! Any other man would have been suspected—any other man would have been guarded, watched, and saved. But in his case, the physicians themselves forgot the ascendancy of the body over the mind. They reckoned him invulnerable even to fever and delirium. In a word, they overlooked the mysterious fellowship of Nature and of Fate,

which levels the strongest with the weakest. The
mistake was most fatal to his country. We have
lost all our greatest—Fox, Pitt, Nelson, Whitbread,
and the poor princess ; but this loss is, in my mind,
the greatest of all. He was so pure, so perfect, so
kind, so true ! Talent in him was so attractive !
Eloquence so useful ! Virtue so commanding !
We shall never have another Sir Samuel Romilly.
I will talk of something else.

When I was telling you some of Mr. Wordsworth's absurdities, did I tell you that he never
dined ? I have just had a letter from Mrs. Hofland,
who has been with her husband to the Lakes, and
spent some days at a Mr. Marshall's, for whom
Mr. H. was painting a picture—but Mrs. Hofland
shall speak for herself :—" On my return from
Mr. M.'s to our Ullswater cottage, I encountered
a friend who condoled with me on the dullness of
my visit. ' Dull ! It was delightful.' ' The long
triste dinners, the breakfasts, the suppers, the
luncheons ! ' ' To be sure fourteen people must
eat, but these said dinners were anything but dull,
I assure you. Why do you call them so ? ' ' Because Mr. and Mrs. Wordsworth were staying
there, and were so overcome by those shocking
meals, that they were forced to come away. The
Wordsworths never dine, you know ; they hate
such doings ; when they are hungry they go to the
cupboard and eat.' And really," observes Mrs.
Hofland, " it is much the best way. There is
Mr. Wordsworth, who will live for a month on cold

beef, and the next on cold bacon ; and my husband will insist on a hot dinner every day. He never thinks how much trouble I have in ordering, nor what a plague my cook is ! " So you see the Wordsworth regimen is likely to spread.

Very sincerely and affectionately yours,

M. R. M.

To Sir William Elford, Bickham, Plymouth

BERTRAM HOUSE, *Dec.* 28, 1818.

MY DEAR FRIEND,

Did I ever mention to you or did you ever hear elsewhere of a Miss Nevinson [Mrs. Gore], poetess, novelist, essayist, and reviewer ? I have just been writing to her in answer to a very kind letter ; but writing in such alarm that I quivered and shook, and looked into the dictionary to see how to spell The, and asked mamma if there were two T's in Tottering. You never saw anybody in such a fright. It was like writing in chains—and now that I am writing to you, for whom I don't care a pin, it 's like a galley-slave let loose from the oar.

Such is my horror of being forced to mind my P's and Q's, to look to my stops and see to my spelling, to be fine and sensible and literary—and so alarming a lady is Miss Nevinson, so sure to put one on the defensive, even when she has no intention to attack. This is no great compliment to my fair correspondent—but it is the truth. Miss Nevinson is a very extraordinary woman ; her conversation (for I don't think very highly of her writings) is perhaps the most dazzling and brilliant that can be imagined.

I have just been reading Hazlitt's *View of the Stage*—a series of critiques originally printed in the different newspapers, particularly the *Chronicle* and the *Examiner*. I had seen most of them before, but I could not help reading them all together ; though so much of Hazlitt is rather dangerous to one's taste—rather like dining on sweetmeats and supping on pickles. So poignant is he, and so rich, everything seems insipid after him. This amusement, great as it always would have been, was very much heightened to me by recollecting so well the first publication of the best articles—those on Kean in the *Morning Chronicle*.[1] I was at Tavistock House at the time, and well remember the doleful visage with which Mr. Perry used to contemplate the long column of criticism, and how he used to execrate " the d—d fellow's d—d stuff " for filling up so much of the paper in the very height of the advertisement season. I shall never forget his long face. It was the only time of the day that I ever saw it either long or sour. He had not the slightest suspicion that he had a man of genius in his pay— not the most remote perception of the merit of the writing—nor the slightest companionship with the author. He hired him, as you hire your footman ;

[1] The belief of the time was that Hazlitt received 1500*l.* from the management of Drury Lane for these articles. They made Kean's reputation and saved the theatre.

and turned him off (with as little or less ceremony
than you would use in discharging the aforesaid
worthy personage) for a very masterly but damaging
critique on Sir Thomas Lawrence, whom Mr. P.,
as one whom he visited and was being painted
by, chose to have praised.   Hazlitt's revenge was
exceedingly characteristic.   Last winter, when his
Characters of Shakespeare and his lectures had
brought him into fashion, Mr. Perry remembered
him as an old acquaintance and asked him to dinner,
and a large party to meet him, to hear him talk, and
to show him off as the lion of the day.   The lion
came—smiled and bowed—handed Miss Bentley
to the dining-room—asked Miss Perry to take
wine—said once " Yes " and twice " No "—and
never uttered another word the whole evening.   The
most provoking part of this scene was, that he was
gracious and polite past all expression—a perfect
pattern of mute elegance—a silent Lord Chester-
field ; and his unlucky host had the misfortune
to be very thoroughly enraged without anything to
complain of.

> Most faithfully and affectionately yours,
> M. R. MITFORD.

To Sir William Elford, Bickham, Plymouth

BERTRAM HOUSE, *Jan.* 9, 1819.

Considering my doleful prognostications, you will
like to know, my dear friend, that I have outlived
the ball, so I must write.   It 's a thing of necessity.

Yes, I am living and " lifelich," as Chaucer says.
And that I did survive that dreaded night, I owe
principally to that charming thing, a dandy. Don't
you like dandies, the beautiful race ? I am sure
you must. But such a dandy as our dandy few
have been fortunate enough to see. In general
they are on a small scale—slim, whipper-snapper
youths, fresh from college—or new mounted on a
dragoon's saddle—dainty light-horse men, or trim
schoolboys. Ours is of a Patagonian breed—six
feet and upwards without his shoes, and broad in
proportion. Unless you have seen a wasp in a solar
microscope you have never seen anything like him.
Perhaps a Brobdingnagian hour-glass might be
more like him still, only I don't think the hour-
glass would be small enough in the waist.

Great as my admiration has always been of the
mechanical inventions of this age, I know nothing
that has given me so high an idea of the power of
machinery—not the Portsmouth Blockhouses, or
the new Mint—as that perfection of mechanism
by which those ribs are endued in those stays. I
think one or two must have been broken, to render
such a compression possible. But it is unjust to
dwell so exclusively on the stays, when every part
of the thing was equally perfect. Trousers—coat
—neckcloth—shirt-collar—head, inside and out—
all were in exact keeping. Every look, every word,
every attitude belonged to those inimitable stays.
Sweet dandy ! I have seen nothing like him since
Liston, in Lord Grizzle. He kept me awake and

alive the whole evening. Dancing or sitting still, he was my " cynosure." I followed him with my eyes as a schoolboy follows the vagaries of his top or the rolling of his hoop. Much and generally as he was admired, I don't think he made so strong an impression on any one as on me. He is even indebted to me for the distinguished attention of a great wit, whose shafts I was lucky enough to direct to that impenetrable target of dandyism. All this he owes to me, and is likely to owe me still—for I am sorry to say my dandy is an ungrateful dandy. Our admiration was by no means mutual. " He had an idea," he said (a very bold assertion by-the-by)—" he had an idea that I was blue-ish." So he scoured away on being threatened with an introduction. Well, peace be to him, poor swain ! and better fortune—for the poor dandy is rather unlucky. He fell into the Thames last summer on a water-party and got wet through his stays ; and this autumn, having affronted a young lady, and being knocked down by her brother, a lad not nineteen, he had the misfortune to fall flat on his back, and was forced to lie till some one came to pick him up, being too strait-laced to help himself.

Adieu, my dear friend. I am always
Most affectionately yours,
M. R. MITFORD.

To Mrs. Hofland

BERTRAM HOUSE, *March* 18, 1819.

Foreseeing an opportunity of sending you a letter
in a few days *via* London (the last note which was
intended to have gone thither by papa getting like
himself, no further on the way than Reading), I
cannot resist thanking you, my dear friend, for your
delightful letter, almost as soon as I have received
it. We are very anxious, too, to hear of your perfect
recovery, as well as Mr. Hofland's—those spring
colds are terrible things, you must take great care
of yourselves. I am very glad my journey is put
off. May makes everybody well. So you have
actually seen Miss —— ! Mr. Hofland's compliments to my portrait painting came just as I was in
a fit of repentance for that very specimen which he
is so good, or so naughty, as to approve. She
wrote to me the plan which was framed at your
house, and her letter was so frank, so hearty, so
irresistibly kind, that my heart smote me for every
saucy thing I had ever said of her. I still agree
with Mr. H. in thinking the picture a good likeness
—she is all that I said, but she is something better
and more. At first sight, she is cold and stiff ;
with those who are unkind to her she is sharp and
cutting ; but you see that when light and air and
warmth are let into her heart, it opens like a flower.
That letter of hers came upon me like a kiss, so
short, so sudden, and so affectionate—you yourself

never wrote a more direct and pressing invitation.
I will never say or think anything saucy of her again,
nor of any one, if I can help it ; and by way of
keeping my resolution, I may as well begin to talk
of a demagogue *par excellence*, Mr. Northmore.
What did I tell you of him in that wee bit of a note
of mine ?   Surely there was not canvas enough for
the man at full length—I could never have done
him justice.   Did I tell you that he was the
Mr. Northmore who was not chosen for Exeter—
the Mr. Northmore who made at Westminster so
notable an oration in favour of the old ass Major
Cartwright — the Mr. Northmore of whom Mr.
Hobhouse said that he had come all the way from
Devonshire to tell people he was a great man at
home ?   Did I tell you he was a talker against time
—loud and shrewd and full of himself, and sharp
all over, from his eagle nose to his pointed boot toe ?
—a perpetual sky-rocket, always bouncing, starting,
and flaming ?—an unremitting volcano, spitting
forth by night and by day smoke, pebbles, cinders,
fire, and all hissing matter ?   Did I tell you all
this ? and did I add that he is a poet ?—author of
a poem which must have appeared incognito, for I
never heard of it ; an epic poem, madam, about
General Washington, to please our American tastes
—an epic in blank verse, which the man has the
conscience to expect me to read and admire ?
You will think he affronted me, but he did not,
except by that modest assurance of his which
affronts everybody—by a certain tone of impertinent

protecting praise which he thought very flattering,
and which gave me a violent fancy to box his ears ;
and by—last and greatest sin—a running accom-
paniment of " very pretty, very pretty, very pretty,"
with which he contrived to render Mrs. D——'s
sweetest song rather worse than inaudible. Now
good-bye, Mr. Northmore—*beau idéal* of a democrat,
I have done with you. He appeared to the greater
disadvantage, too, from being accompanied by one
of the most interesting old men in the world—a
Northumberland man—an old friend of our family
—one of those venerable persons who make age
so lovely and so lovable ; mild, cheerful, kind, and
wise—smiling as brightly as my own dear father, and
talking just as Izaak Walton would have talked if
one had gone out fishing with him. I do wish you
had seen Mr. J——. By-the-way, I picked up a
great many stories from him. He lives at Marlow,
and is exceedingly intimate with Peacock and
Shelley, and acquainted with all the new school.
He says the system of plunder exercised upon poor
Mr. Shelley exceeds all belief. Leigh Hunt went
to Marlow once for money, and finding Mr. S.
without any family, took off a load of the good man's
furniture—chairs and tables and bedsteads ! Is it
not incredible ? And Mr. Godwin, his papa-in-
law, was much worse ; he used to threaten to stab
himself if his dutiful son-in-law would not accept
his bills. Only fancy him down on his knees,
flourishing a drawn dagger and talking tragedy !
It 's really better than " Tom Thumb." But it was

no joke to poor Mr. Shelley. He used to send for
Mr. Peacock to protect him, and is fairly gone
abroad to get rid of this fine grand sort of sentimental persecution. Well, great authors are great
people—but I believe they are best seen at a distance. The Alps are only fit for the background of
a picture, and not always for that. In the mean-
time, we may amuse ourselves with their books.
Pray, have you read a Scotch novel called *Marriage*?[1]
If not, pray do. It's the very book for an invalid,
so very laughable and nothing else. There are
three Scotch old maids and their married friend,
who are just what novel personages ought to be,
very new in books, and very old in nature. These
are the cream certainly, but there is a great deal of
comic talent throughout, and there had need.
Nothing but the buoyant air-bladder of comedy
would ever have floated the preaching and prosing
of the second volume—in total want of interest from
beginning to end, the interminable speeches, and
that deadest of dead weights, the all perfect heroine.
That is the heaviest millstone of all. A book laden
with an impeccable heroine ought to be covered
all over with cork jackets, not to sink. Somebody
has said that we never forgive perfection unless it
be made thoroughly wretched. Now this damsel
is not wretched in the least, she is a female Sir
Charles Grandison, with no trials but the show off
trials of duty—no cares but the tender cares of love.
How I do hate those over-good book-people !

[1] By Miss Ferrier.

They are just like triple refined sugar—sweet and bright and hard and spotless, and good for nothing till united with some ardent spirit or some powerful acid. Luckily I know how to skip (invaluable art, I wonder no one has written an essay on it), and Miss Grizzy and Miss Jacky make ample amends for the fair Mary's sins of wisdom and virtue. Grizzy's letters are past all praise—I prefer them even to Jacky's. Here am I talking of Miss N——, and Mr. Northmore, and novels, and such like baubles, and entirely forgetting the fine opportunity I have to show off, and look wise and grand, and critical and classical, and bluer than a blue bag. Mr. —— has finished his translations —those translations which have been forty years in hand—from Dante, Tasso, Ariosto, Petrarch, Ovid, and Virgil ; and he has chosen me for his critic and auditress, upon the same principle, I suppose, that Molière chose his old woman. They only want *my* last revisal (there's for you !) to be printed at his private press ; that is to say, twelve copies thrown off there, and these are sent to London, by way of MS., to be finely printed by John Valpy. This will strike you as much such a *cheap* plan as his Grace the Duke of Marlborough might pursue in a similar occasion—but money is of no consequence at ——. The translations are singularly fine—true to the words and spirit of the originals—and yet most purely English in their fine diction and their sweet and flowing versification. The " Ugolino " and " Isabella " stories are superb.

Those Italian people were my old and dear acquaintance. I can't say I was quite so intimate with the Latin gentlemen. I had read Dryden's *Virgil*, to be sure—but it was a long time ago—and Mr. Ovid I had never met with in my life. I have now had the honour of an introduction to his tale of Phæton, and I think him a very fine fellow indeed. He beats even Mr. Southey for magnificent nonsense, *Kehama* is pale and faded pink, compared to the glowing scarlet of the *Metamorphoses*.   Virgil I dare not presume to praise. The voice of all the world has given him his rank in Parnassus ; but I may safely quarrel with one whom there is no injuring, and to be sure, that fourth *Æneid* would make any worm-feminine that crawls on the earth turn against him. That intolerable rascal, the pious Æneas ! That abominable fool, the tender Dido ! My dear Mrs. Hofland, I have no patience with the man. He does not deserve such a translator as Mr. —— ; he deserves only such an one as Mr. Beresford (the misery man [1]), who has produced, without knowing it, a travestie more perfect than Cotton's. *E.g.* In the midst of Dido's fine passion, where she talks of scattering the limbs of her faithless lover on the sea, of immolating his son, of slaying his followers, and so forth, Mr. Beresford makes her say, very quietly, " Why should I not kill the young Ascanius, and *dish him* to his sire ? " And all Oxford and half Cambridge subscribed to this translation ? I don't suppose there is so fine

[1] Author of the *Miseries of Human Life*.

a stroke even in " Washington," that masterpiece
of Mr. ——'s heroics.

What could Mrs. J—— possibly say to you,
my dear friend, to render forgiveness necessary ?
Something very hard, I am sure—very rude—very
officious. Do tell me what. I have a notion this
Mrs. J—— can be a little alarming sometimes.
Mrs. C—— once, in telling a long rigmarole story,
gave a bit of a picture of her which I have never
forgotten. She was speaking of a morning visit
in Cumberland Place, where she was with Miss
J—— and another lady, " and then," quoth she,
" just as we were at our merriest, in sailed Madam
J——, like a tragedy queen, scolded us all round,
silenced us, and put us to flight." My Miss J——
always speaks of her mother with a respect and
affection which does great credit to herself, but I
have no doubt that she can be disagreeable enough.
I only wish she may take it into her head to give
me a scolding. I have a snug little taste for im-
pertinence, which I make it a point of conscience
not to indulge unprovoked, but which it quite does
me good to let loose when I see occasion : so that
those who, presuming on a very undeserved character for gentleness and so forth, which I have got,
Heaven knows how, undertake to preach to me,
sometimes find themselves turned round in a very
unexpected manner. Now, I take Mrs. J—— to
be a person whom I should really like to toss. Do
tell me what she said to you. I foresee I shall be
obliged to give her a taste of my quality—only I

should be sorry to vex her charming daughter. So you think this scourging will do Haydon good ! I do not. I am no disciplinarian ; in my mind whipping is bad both for man and boy, and you should remember that in this present case the rod has been tried pretty often with no remarkably dulcifying power. In short, *he* is himself the best authority, and I had a letter from him just after the first burst of success attending this exhibition, in which, with his characteristic *naïveté*, he talks of this gleam of prosperity as having softened him, and made him so good, that he forgave all his enemies, and even wished to lessen their mortification. And he is right—metaphysically right—in my opinion. Prosperity does sweeten, and Adversity does harden and fire up a noble character. The spoilt children of Fortune are generally more amiable, kinder, better-tempered than those whom she has cast aside. I know that this is just the reverse of the prevailing sentiment, which holds that misfortune is good for the mind, etc., etc.; but I don't mind a little opposition, as you know of old. I like to be in a select minority. Talking of minorities, I shall be delighted to behold Mr. Hobhouse. The very sight of him marching down his garden, opening the little gate, turning into the road, will be a pleasure to me. To gaze on Mr. Hobhouse, I shall actually be guilty of the missy iniquity of watching at the window. This is not merely because he is Lord Byron's friend—not at all, indeed—but because he is Napoleon's defender.

" Elle est folle de Buonaparte," Mr. D—— says
of me, and the madness I am afraid is rather increasing than diminishing. But he is no common
man this Mr. Hobhouse ; accomplished, enlight-
ened, firm, honest, bold—an author, an orator,
and a man of fashion, who dares exile himself from
his caste ; who becomes, voluntarily as it were, a
pariah, rather than betray the cause of the people.
I have a great respect for Mr. Hobhouse. He is,
I hear, to marry Miss Susan Burdett—the beauty,
and the favourite. I believe this is certain.

Reading is in a great bustle of joy and triumph
at Mr. Palmer's success. I am very glad myself—
the man is a good sort of man (though I hate
pensions), and, moreover, very useful as a franker
in this unparliamentary neighbourhood. But the
pension is a pension for all that. My politics are
very unaccommodating ; I cannot give up principles for men, not even for an intimate friend.
You shall see the comedy, but you must not expect
too much. It is as compared to very witty and
humorous dramas, as a water-colour drawing to an
oil picture. There is but one attempt at a comic
character, and that attempt is a failure ; neither is
it at all sentimental. It is, rather tender, rather
lively, rather delicate, and rather tiresome. This
is a very true and impartial character. As to
writing a novel, I can't, I wish I could ; nothing I
should like better, it must be so amusing. I have
begun two, and got on very well as long as I stuck
to landscape and portrait painting ; but when I

was obliged to make my pictures walk out of their
frames and speak for themselves, when I came to
the action, I was foundered. In short, I lacked
invention, so both my novels went into the fire,
where I most heartily wish all my poems were
keeping them company. It is not because Mr.
Gifford abused me that I do not write, but because
Mr. Gifford's abuse happened, for once in his life,
to be right. Now, I don't say this to make you
contradict me, and say civil things, but because I
really feel it to be the truth, and beg of you not to
say another word on the subject. I believe I ought
to be very thoroughly ashamed of this quantity
of nonsense, but you have persuaded me that my
" chitter chatter " amuses you, and must take the
consequences of your civility. I hope nobody
ever hears a word except Mr. Hofland, of whose
indulgence I am so secure. Kindest regards to
him and to you from all here, not forgetting the
lovely boy. Get well, and write and tell me so.
Adieu, my dear friend.

    P.S.—I hope this sad influenza has not put a stop
to the Cumberland Cottage. I have set my heart on
seeing that the glory of the Academy. Who is the
man that has abused Mr. Haydon ? Do you know ?
Is it the author of the *Catalogue Raisonné*—and
who is the author of the *Catalogue Raisonné* ? I
did know, but I have forgotten.

To Sir William Elford, Bickham, Plymouth

BERTRAM HOUSE, *May* 30, 1819.

Papa having made Mr. Dundas promise and re-promise not to transmogrify you into a lady (as once before happened, you know, my dear friend), I avail myself of his obliging offer to transmit to you " these presents." How charming is the new volume of Horace Walpole's letters ! He was, beyond doubt, the best letter-writer of his day—better than Gray—better than Cowper. You and I thought so always. I do not think very highly of Madame D'Arblay's books. The style is so strutting. She does so stalk about on Dr. Johnson's old stilts. What she says wants so much translating into common English, and when translated would seem so common-place, that I have always felt strongly tempted to read all the serious parts with my fingers' ends.

Lady Pitt's death has added a thousand a year to the Duke of Wellington's new estate. This great captain of ours is a prodigiously lucky man. Besides the property, he gets a very pretty place, finely situated.

Ever most affectionately yours,

M. R. MITFORD.

To Sir William Elford, Bickham, Plymouth

BERTRAM HOUSE, *June* 29, 1819.

A novel should be as like life as a painting, but not as like life as a piece of waxwork. Madame D'Arblay has much talent, but no taste. She degrades her heroines in every possible way, bodily and mental. All her heroines—nothing can exceed her impartiality in this respect—Cecilia, Evelina, Camilla, and Juliette, all go into cowhouses and keep bad company. She has no touch of Cæsar's nicety about her. Another fault, which I think I have mentioned before, is the sameness of her characters; they all say one thing twenty times over. In some Russian travels—I don't remember whether Dr. Clarke's or Sir H. K. Porter's—there is an account of a concert of wind instruments performed by an almost countless number of vassals of some great lord, each of whose instruments has but one single note, so that the living machines form themselves the entire musical scale. Now Madame D'Arblay's characters are like these vassals. They have but one note.

I had the other day a letter from Mrs. Hofland, who, in the midst of a long critique on the pictures in the Exhibition, speaks thus of a certain landscape of your acquaintance: " Sir W. E.'s picture is a very beautiful natural scene, most beautifully and honestly painted—not slipped over like a white-washer, as Mr. Turner does things, and as your favourite, Mr. Wordsworth, writes poems " (by-the-by, Mrs. Hofland is mistaken there—Wordsworth is the highest finisher of any poet going) ; " but done as if the thing was worth doing—as I take it everything should be, if done at all."

Most affectionately yours,

M. R. MITFORD.

To Sir William Elford, Bickham, Plymouth

BERTRAM HOUSE, *Jan.* 30, 1820.

I have just heard that the King is dead. Poor venerable old man ! It is fortunate for you that my paper is nearly filled and the servant waiting to take my letter into Reading, or I should have vented to you some of that fulness of thought and feeling which such an event forces into every mind.

Jan. 31.

I wish in good earnest that you would set about writing a novel. Do try. I began a novel myself once, and got on very prosperously for about a hundred pages of character and description. You would have liked it, I think, for it was very light and airy, and laughed, with some success, at my hero and heroine, and myself, and my readers. I came to a dead stop for want of invention. A lack of incident killed the poor thing. It went out like a candle. In all those hundred pages not one person had said a single word or done a single thing but my heroine : and she—guess what she had done ! Turned the lock of a drawing-room door ! After this it was time to give up novel-writing.

Did you, my dear friend, ever happen to read Mr. Thomas Hope's book about furniture ? Or do you happen to recollect (which will do just as well) the famous quizzing the said book met with in the *Edinburgh Review* ? The book itself seemed

to me, when I saw it in a fine presentation copy,
all scarlet and gold, to be a grand piece of furniture
itself, and one as little made to be read as a chair or
a table. Well, this Mr. Thomas Hope has, they
say, written *Anastasius*. The *New Monthly Magazine* says so ; but that 's rather an argument against
the fact, inasmuch as the *New Monthly Magazine*
does certainly, assertion for assertion, tell more lies
than truths ; but Lady Madalina Palmer says so
on good authority ; so that this incredible fact must
be believed. Perhaps I am talking Greek to you
all this time, and you have not read *Anastasius*.
Well, then, it 's a book which, but for this testimony,
I should from internal evidence have attributed at
once to that prince of wickedness and poetry, Lord
Byron. It 's altogether Grecian ; is not that like
Lord Byron ? It 's exceedingly sceptical ; is not
that like Lord Byron ? It complains of a jealous
wife ; is not that like Lord Byron ? It is full of fine
and gloomy poetry (in prose), which is of the very
same style with Lord Byron's. It is still fuller of
the light derisive mockery—the tossing about of all
good feeling, so gibing and so Voltaire-ish, which
no one could or would do but Lord Byron. It is a
most uncomfortable book—is not that like Lord
Byron ? And lastly, it is all full of the sneering
misanthropic wretched author ; is not that Lord
Byron ? If not written by him, it is certainly in
his character ; and a very powerful work it is for
good and for evil—a sort of Eastern *Gil Blas*—only
bloodier, longer, less attractive. I shall remember

it all my days ; but I shall never think of reading
it again.

Have you in your neighbourhood any infant
prodigies ?   I have had the honour to be introduced
to one lately—a little miss of seven years old, who is
in training for a blue stocking, and is indeed, as far
as pedantry and self-conceit and ignorance go, quite
worthy of the title already.   I have heard of this
poor little girl off and on any time these two years.
They told me she knew by heart all *Richard*, all
Macbeth, all *Twelfth Night*, all Virgil's *Æneid*, and.
Tressan's *Mythology*—a pretty selection for a child,
is it not ?   On examination, the perilous part of
the knowledge flew off.   She had by rote about
six lines of the witches—three of Richard's first
soliloquy—none at all of *Twelfth Night* ; had never
heard of Dido, and called Juno a man.   But then
the poor little thing was as unnatural and artificial
as if she were really a second edition of the Admirable Crichton ; played at no sport but the intellectual
games of chess and dumb crambo ; was pert and
pale, and peaked and priggish—a perfect " old
woman cut shorter," and the very reverse of the
romping roly-poly thing, as round and blooming as
a rose, and almost as silly, which is my *beau idéal*
of a child of that age.   How much I abhor anything
out of season !   And how much I pitied this poor
little girl !   She is the only child of a very clever
and ambitious mother, delighting in distinction
of all sorts ; and there has been the child's misfortune.   I hope to see Mrs. Dickinson's little girl

a perfect pattern of childish beauty, simplicity, silliness, mischief, idleness, and ignorance ; these being, in my opinion, the very best foundations for a clever woman.

Ever most affectionately yours,

M. R. MITFORD.

To Sir William Elford, Bickham, Plymouth

THREE MILE CROSS, *April* 12, 1822.

I thank you very much, my dear Sir William, for your very kind and entertaining letter. The story of the housemaid and the picture is delicious ; and I enter into it the more thoroughly, from having lately rescued some blotted papers of my own from the fangs of an animal of that species. My dramatic scene looked, as she said, such a " tatterdemalion piece of scribble," that she clawed it up in her paw, much as a monkey would seize on an open letter, and was actually proceeding to light a fire withal, when I snatched my precious manuscript from her devouring fangs. I wish you had seen the look of contempt with which this damsel of ours—a *ci-devant* schoolmistress—looked at my composition ! I dare say she would have whipped any one of her scholars that wrote only half as ill.

Now, what shall I talk about ? We have got Mrs. Opie's new novel of *Madeline* in the house, but I have not opened it yet. One knows the usual ingredients of her tales just as one knows the component parts of a plum-pudding. So much

common sense (for the flour) ; so much vulgarity
(for the suet) ; so much love (for the sugar) ; so
many songs (for the plums) ; so much wit (for the
spices) ; so much fine binding morality (for the
eggs) ; and so much mere mawkishness and in-
sipidity (for the milk and water wherewith the said
pudding is mixed up).   I think she has left off being
pathetic—at least I have left out that quality in my
enumeration.   Yet she is a very clever woman, and
a good-natured woman ; and though my exceeding
fastidiousness with respect to style and elegance
and gracefulness in writing deprives me of any
pleasure in her works, there are a great many very
good judges who admire her writings greatly.   I
hope you won't tell her this by way of a compliment,
though I have lately met with a misadventure which
would go near to tying one's pen down to its good
behaviour all one's life.   A discreet correspondent
of mine (female, of course) inquired my opinion of
a recent publication.   I wrote her a very fair
character of the work (which I did not very much
admire)—a fair and candid character, with just
enough of sweet to flavour the sour (like sugar in
mint sauce).   It was not a sweeping, knock-me-
down critique—but a light, airy, neatly-feathered
shaft—whose censure looked almost like praise.
So much the worse for me.   My goose of a correspondent took it for complimentary ; and, by way
of recommending me to the author of the cut-up
work, fairly read him the passage out of my letter,
and then in her reply gravely told me what she had

done ! Of course she will never get any but how-d' ye-do letters from me again as long as she lives.

To confess the truth, my dear friend, I am so thoroughly out of heart about *Foscari* that I cannot bear even to think or speak on the subject. Never-theless the drama is my talent—my only talent—and I mean to go on and improve. I *will* improve —that is my fixed determination. Can you re-commend me a good subject for an historical tragedy ? I wish you would think of this, and if you have none in your own mind, ask any likely person. It should have *two* prominent male parts —and I should prefer an Italian story in the four-teenth, fifteenth, sixteenth, or seventeenth century, as affording most scope, and being less liable to blame for any deviation from truth in the plot than any well-known incident in the greater States. I once thought of our Charles the First. He and Cromwell would form two very finely-contrasted characters — but the facts are too well-known. Farewell, my dear friend.

Ever most sincerely and affectionately yours,

M. R. MITFORD.

To B. R. Haydon, Esq., Paddington Green

THREE MILE CROSS, *August* 24, 1823.

Pray are you a cricketer ? We are very great ones—I mean our parish, of which we, the feminine members, act audience, and " though we do not play, o'erlook the balls." When I wrote to you

last I was just going to see a grand match in a fine
old park near us, Bramshill, between Hampshire,
with Mr. Budd, and All England. I anticipated
great pleasure from so grand an exhibition, and
thought, like a simpleton, the better the play the
more the enjoyment. Oh, what a mistake ! There
they were—a set of ugly old men, whiteheaded and
baldheaded (for half of Lord's was engaged in the
combat, players and gentlemen, Mr. Ward and
Lord Frederick, the veterans of the green) dressed
in tight white jackets (the Apollo Belvidere could
not bear the hideous disguise of a cricketing
jacket), with neckcloths primly tied round their
throats, fine japanned shoes, silk stockings, and
gloves, instead of our fine village lads, with their
unbuttoned collars, their loose waistcoats, and the
large shirt-sleeves which give an air so picturesque
and Italian to their glowing, bounding youthfulness :
there they stood, railed in by themselves, silent,
solemn, slow—playing for money, making a business of the thing, grave as judges, taciturn as chess
players—a sort of dancers without music, instead
of the glee, the fun, the shouts, the laughter, the
glorious confusion of the country game. And there
were we, the lookers-on, in tents and marquees, fine
and freezing, dull as the players, cold as this hard
summer weather, shivering and yawning and trying
to seem pleased, the curse of gentility on all our
doings, as stupid as we could have been in a ball-
room. I never was so much disappointed in my
life. But everything is spoilt when money puts its

ugly nose in. To think of playing cricket for hard
cash ! Money and gentility would ruin any pastime
under the sun. Much to my comfort (for the
degrading my favourite sport into a " science," as
they were pleased to call it, had made me quite
spiteful) the game ended unsatisfactorily to all
parties, winners and losers. Old Lord Frederick,
on some real or imaginary affront, took himself off
in the middle of the second innings, so that the two
last were played without him, by which means his
side lost, and the other could hardly be said to win.
So be it always when men make the noble game of
cricket an affair of bettings and hedgings, and,
may be, of cheatings.

And now God bless you ! Kindest regards and
best wishes from all.

> Ever yours,
> M. R. MITFORD.

To Sir William Elford

THREE MILE CROSS, *March* 5, 1824.

MY DEAR FRIEND,

In spite of your prognostics, I think you will like
Our Village. It will be out in three weeks or a
month ; and it will be an obligation if you will cause
it to be asked for at circulating libraries, &c. It is
not one connected story, but a series of sketches of
country manners, scenery, and character, with some
story intermixed, and connected by unity of locality
and of purpose. It is exceedingly playful and

lively, and I think you will like it. Charles Lamb (the matchless " Elia " of the *London Magazine*) says that nothing so fresh and characteristic has appeared for a long while. It is not over modest to say this ; but who would not be proud of the praise of such a *proser* ? And as you, in common with all sensible people, like light reading, I say again that you will like it.

Pray have you read the American novels ? I mean the series by Mr. Cooper—*The Spy*, &c. If you have not, send for them, and let me hear the result. In my mind they are as good as anything Sir Walter Scott ever wrote. He has opened fresh ground, too (if one may say so of the sea). No one but Smollett has ever attempted to delineate the naval character ; and then he is so coarse and hard. Now this has the same truth and power, with a deep, grand feeling. I must not overpraise it, for fear of producing the reaction which such injudicious enthusiasm is calculated to induce ; but I must request you to read it. Only read it. Imagine the author's boldness in taking Paul Jones for a hero, and his power in making one care for him ! I envy the Americans their Mr. Cooper. Tell me how you like *The Pilot*. There is a certain Long Tom who appears to me the finest thing since Parson Adams. God bless you, my dear friend !

Ever very sincerely yours,

M. R. MITFORD.

To Sir William Elford, Bickham, Plymouth

THREE MILE CROSS, *June* 23, 1824.

MY DEAR FRIEND,

I am quite delighted that you like my book. Your notion of letters pleases me much, as I see plainly that it is the result of the old prepossessions and partialities, which do me so much honour and give me so much pleasure. But it would never have done. The sketches are too long, and necessarily too much connected, for *real* correspondence ; and as to anything make-believe, it has been my business to keep that out of sight as much as possible. Besides which, we are free and easy in these days, and talk to the public as a friend. Read *Elia*, or the *Sketch Book*, or Hazlitt's *Table Talk*, or any popular book of the new school, and you will find that we have turned over the Johnsonian periods and the Blair-ian formality to keep company with the wigs and hoops, the stiff curtseys and low bows of our ancestors. In short, my dear friend, letters are now-a-days more the vehicles of kindness, and less of wit than they used to be. It was very convenient, when people who wrote books were forced to put stiff stays on them, to have a sort of dishabille for the mind as well as for the body, and to write a letter as they put on a *robe de chambre*. But now the periodical press takes charge of those bursts of gaiety and criticism which the post was wont to receive ; and the public—the reading public

—is, as I said before, the correspondent and con-
fidant of everybody.

Having thus made the best defence I can against
your criticism, I proceed to answer your question,
" Are the characters and descriptions true ? "
Yes ! yes ! yes ! As true as is well possible. You,
as a great landscape painter, know that in painting
a favourite scene you do a little embellish, and can't
help it ; you avail yourself of happy accidents of
atmosphere, and if anything be ugly, you strike it
out, or if anything be wanting, you put it in. But
still the picture is a likeness ; and that this is a very
faithful one, you will judge when I tell you that a
worthy neighbour of ours, a post captain, who has
been in every quarter of the globe, and is equally
distinguished for the sharp look-out and the *bonhomie* of his profession, accused me most seriously
of carelessness in putting " The Rose " for " The
Swan," as the sign of our next-door neighbour ;
and was no less disconcerted at the *misprint* (as he
called it) of B for R in the name of our next town.
A cela près, he declares the picture to be exact.
Nevertheless, I do not expect to be poisoned.
Why should I ? I have said no harm of my neighbours, have I ? The great danger would be that
my dear friend Joel might be spoilt ; but I take
care to keep the book out of our pretty Harriet's
way ; and so I hope that that prime ornament of
our village will escape the snare for his vanity which
the seeing so exact a portrait of himself in a printed
book might occasion.

By-the-way, the names of the villagers are true—
of the higher sketches they are feigned, of course.
But I will give my dear Miss Elford, who seems
interested in knowing the exact state of the case, a
key. Her note is charming. I never saw a more
beautiful simplicity ; and when she speaks of her
sister, it is quite enchanting to see how the love
breaks out. Yes ! I shall give her the key, and
will only thank you, in the first place, for promoting
the sale ; and tell you, in the second, that it sells
well, and has been received by the literary world,
and reviewed in all the literary papers, &c., better
than I, for modesty, dare to say. God bless you,
my dear friend !

Always most sincerely and affectionately yours,

M. R. MITFORD.

To the Rev. William Harness, Hampstead

THREE MILE CROSS, *Wednesday, Oct. 9, 1825.*

MY DEAR FRIEND,

Although I have no member under hand, I write
without waiting the uncertain chance of meeting
with one—first, to thank you for your very kind
attention about the money—secondly, to give you
all the information I myself possess respecting the
play. Mr. Kemble found *Charles* on his table on
his return from abroad—read it immediately—
thought it " admirable though somewhat dangerous "—and sent it at once to the licenser. For
three weeks we heard nothing of it. At last came

a note from Mr. Colman to say " that, in consequence of the exceedingly delicate nature of the
subject and incidents of *Charles the First*, he had
received instructions to send the MS. to the Lord
Chamberlain, that he might himself judge, on
perusal, of the safety of granting a license." Accordingly the piece is gone to the Duke of Montrose,
who is in Scotland. And there we stand. Is not
this very strange and unusual ?

Have you read Pepys's Memoirs ? I am extremely diverted by them, and prefer them to
Evelyn's, all to nothing. He was too precise and
too gentlemanly and too sensible by half ;—wrote
in full dress, with an eye, if not to the press, at least
to posthumous reputation. Now this man sets
down his thoughts in a most becoming dishabille—
does not care twopence for posterity ; and evidently
thinks wisdom a very foolish thing. I don't know
when any book has amused me so much. It is
the very perfection of gossiping—most relishing
nonsense.

How long do you stay at Hampstead ? I shall
tell you the fate of *Charles* as soon as I know it.
Do let me know what you think of Mr. Fitzharris.
Kindest love to dear Mary.—Mamma's to all of
you. Ever, my dear friend,

Most sincerely yours,

M. R. MITFORD.

To Miss Jephson, Hatfield, Herts

THREE MILE CROSS, *Friday, Oct.* 30, 1829.

Did I tell you that it is the scarlet potentilla, which sells at fifteen shillings, being manufactured (I don't know how) out of the *Potentilla Formosa* and running from the colour when propagated by seed. *Our* plant, which is quite as pretty—prettier, I think—hardy and generous both in seed and root —will be an established garden flower, like pinks and roses, and always a pet with me for your sake, dearest, and for Mr. Wordsworth's. Don't let us forget to send you some seed from the Rydal Mount plant next season.

I have had a magnificent present of greenhouse plants, chiefly geraniums—a whole cartload—and am at present labouring under *l'embarras des richesses*, not being sure whether even the genius of Clarke will make the greenhouse hold them. *À propos* to that astrologer, I have got the ephemeris. Marianne finding even Mrs. Scott fail, took heart at last and applied to Captain Kater ; who, being himself a demi-semi believer, has lent us the identical thing for our purpose, in the shape of an almanac published by order of the Board of Longitude. Between ourselves, I believe it 's the identical Board of Longitude copy, from which, he says, a horoscope can be framed with the most perfect nicety and exactness. I have not seen Clarke since I obtained this treasure, but am expecting him every day.

Now, my dearest, I am going to tell you of an exploit of mine which I longed for you extremely to share. Last Saturday I dined out, and was reproached by a young fox-hunter with never having seen the hounds throw off. I said I should like the sight. The lady of the house said she would drive me some day. The conversation dropped, and I never expected to hear more of it. The next day, however, Sir John Cope (the master of the hounds) calling on my friend, the thing was mentioned and settled ; and the young man who originally suggested the matter rode over to let me know that at half-past nine the next day our friend would call for me. At half-past nine, accordingly, she came in a little limber pony-carriage drawn by a high-blooded little mare, whom she herself (the daughter and sister of a whole race of fox-hunters) had been accustomed to hunt in Wiltshire, and attended by her husband's hunting-groom excel- lently mounted.

The day was splendid and off we set. It was the first day of the season. The hounds were to meet in Bramshill Park, Sir John Cope's old place ; and it was expected to be the greatest field and most remarkable day of many seasons ; Mr. Warde, the celebrated fox-hunter—the very Nestor of the field, who, after keeping fox-hounds for fifty-seven years, has just, at seventy-nine, found himself growing old and given them up—was on a visit at the house, and all the hunt were likely to assemble to see this delightful person ; certainly the pleasantest old man that it ever has been my fortune to foregather with—more beautiful than my father, and in the same style.

Well, off we set—got to Bramshill just as breakfast was over—saw the hounds brought out in front of the house—drove to cover—saw the fox found, and the first grand burst at his going off—followed him to another covert, and the scent being bad and the field so numerous, that he was constantly headed back, both he, who finally ran to earth, and another fox found subsequently, kept dodging about from wood to wood in that magnificent demesne—the very perfection of park scenery, hill and dale, and wood and water—and for about four hours, we with our spirited pony, kept up with the chase, driving about over road and no road, across ditches and through gaps, often run away with, sometimes almost tossed out, but with a degree of delight and enjoyment such as I never felt before, and never, I verily believe, shall feel again. The field (above a hundred horsemen, most of them the friends of my fair companion) were delighted with our sportsmanship, which in me was unexpected ; they showed us the kindest attention—brought me the brush—and when, at three o'clock, we and Mr. Warde and one or two others went into luncheon, whilst the hounds went on to Eversley, I really do not believe that there was a gentleman present ungratified by our gratification. Unless you have seen such a scene you can hardly imagine its animation or its beauty. The horses are most beautiful,

and the dogs, although not pretty separately, are
so when collected and in their own scenery ; which
is also exactly the case with the fox-hunters' scarlet
coats.

I had seen nothing of the park before, beyond the
cricket-ground, and never could have had such a
guide to its inmost recesses—the very heart of its
sylvan solitudes—as the fox. The house—a superb
structure of Elizabeth's day, in proud repair—is
placed on so commanding an eminence that it
seemed meeting us in every direction, and harmon-
ized completely with the old English feeling of the
park and the sport. You must see Bramshill. It
is like nothing hereabouts, but reminds me of the
grand Gothic castles in the north of England—
Chillingham, Alnwick, &c. It was the residence
of Prince Henry, James the First's eldest son, and
is worthy his memory. It has a haunted room,
shut up and full of armour ; a chest where they say
a bride hid herself on her wedding-day, and the
spring-lock closing, was lost and perished, and never
found until years and years had passed (this story,
by-the-way, is common to old houses ; it was told
me of the great house at Malsanger) ; swarms with
family pictures ; has a hall with the dais ; much
fine tapestry ; and, in short, is wanting in no point
of antique dignity. The Duke of Wellington went
to look at it as adjoining his own estate and suiting
his station ; but he unwilling, I believe, to lose the
interest of so much capital, made the characteristic
reply that Strathfieldsaye was good enough for the

duchess, and that he saw nothing to admire at Bramshill except Sir John's pretty housekeeper. I am sure Sir John is much fitter for the master of Bramshill, with his love of cricket, his hospitality, and his fox-hounds, than the Duke with all his fame.

God bless you ! Tell me when you come, and how long you stay.

Ever yours, in galloping fox-hunter's haste,

M. R. M.

To Miss Sedgwick's niece, U.S.A.

THREE MILE CROSS, *Jan.* 1835.

MY DEAR YOUNG FRIEND,

I am very much obliged for your kind enquiries respecting the people in my book. It is much to be asked about by a little lady on the other side of the Atlantic, and we are very proud of it accordingly.

" Mag " was a real greyhound, and everything told of her was literally true ; but alas ! she is no more. Harriet and Joel are not married yet ; you shall have the very latest intelligence of her. I am expecting two or three friends to dinner, and she is making an apple-tart and custards, which I wish with all my heart that you and your aunt were coming to partake of.

The rest of the people are all doing well in their several ways, and I am always, my dear little girl,

Most sincerely yours,

M. R. MITFORD

To Dr. Mitford, Three Mile Cross

56 RUSSELL SQUARE, *May* 26, 1836.

Mr. Wordsworth, Mr. Landor, and Mr. White dined here.   I like Mr. Wordsworth of all things ; he is a most venerable-looking old man, delightfully mild and placid, and most kind to me.   Mr. Landor is a very striking-looking person, and exceedingly clever.   Also we had a Mr. Browning, a young poet (author of *Paracelsus*), and Mr. Proctor, and Mr. Chorley, and quantities of poets, &c.   Stanfield and Lucas were also there, and young Brown, Lord Jeffrey's nephew, who says that he misses you beyond description.   Archdeacon Wrangham is not in London.   Mr. Willis has sailed for America. Mr. Moore and Miss Edgeworth are not in town.

Mr. Crabb Robinson is to come and have a gossip with me to-morrow.   We *had* a pretty good gossip to-night.   We meet Henry Hope and Mr. Dyce, amongst others, to-morrow, at William Harness's. Henry Hope, they say here, has 80,000*l.* per annum —a pretty little income !—and is just as unaffected as he was when we saw him there.   You cannot think how much I like Ellen Tree and Stanfield ; so would you.

There was a curious affair to-night : all the sergeants went to the play [1] in a body, and sat in one box, except Mr. Sergeant Wilde, who had a box for himself and family.   Lord Grey and his family were in a private box just opposite to us ;

[1] To see Sergeant Talfourd's *Ion.*

and the house was filled with people of that class in the boxes, and the pit crammed with gentlemen. Very, very gratifying, was it not ?

God bless you, my own dearest dear ! I am tired to death, and must go to bed.

I have just had your dear letter, and rejoice to find that you are so well. I will write to-morrow, and tell you all the news of the day.

Mr. Sergeant has forgotten to bring me a frank, and I am full of bustle.

Heaven bless you, my dearest ! Love to dear, dear Dash.

Ever faithfully yours,
M. R. MITFORD.

To Dr. Mitford, Three Mile Cross

RUSSELL SQUARE, *May* 28 and 29, 1836.

MY DEAREST FATHER,

Our dinner at Mr. Kenyon's (to which I went with the Harnesses) was magnificent. Mr. Wordsworth, whom I *love*—he is an adorable old man— Mr. Landor—who is as splendid a person as Mr. Kenyon, but not so full of sweetness and sympathy—the charming Miss Barrett, Mr. Courtenay, and three or four more, came to dinner ; one of the most magnificent dinners I ever saw ; a much finer house and finer style than while Mrs. Kenyon lived.

Miss Barrett has translated the most difficult of the Greek plays (the *Prometheus Bound*), and written most exquisite poems in almost every style. She is so sweet and gentle, and so pretty, that one looks at her as if she were some bright flower ; and she says it is like a dream that she should be talking to me, whose works she knows by heart. You cannot imagine how very, very, very kindly Mr. Wordsworth speaks of my poor works. You, who know what I think of him, can imagine how much I am gratified by his praise. I find that half the literary world is invited to meet me at Lady Dacre's.

To Dr. Mitford, Three Mile Cross

RUSSELL SQUARE, *May* 30, 1836.

My darling will have found from my letters how we go on. Jerrold was here last night, and White, Crabb Robinson, Mr. Landor, Mr. Kenyon, Mr. Shepherd, Mr. Maule, and a thousand beside ; and to-day first came Mrs. Lewis, and then, pre- cisely at one, the Duke of Devonshire. He brought me a splendid nosegay of lilies of the valley (a thousand flowers without leaves—I hope I shall find mine in their prime) and moss roses, and stayed above two hours. You would hardly believe that Mrs. Talfourd came and sprawled and bawled, but could not make him hear. I *did*, most com- fortably ; and he must have been pleased, for he begged me never to come to London again without giving him the opportunity of enjoying a similar pleasure. Gave me an order to see Chiswick (containing, as he said, *that* most interesting to me —pictures and flowers), and regretted that he could not show it to me himself at present, which some day or other, he said, he hoped to do.

Then came Mr. Otley, then Lady Mary Shepherd and some more people, whom you don't know; and then I went out to Mr. Barrett's, and to William Harness's, and to call upon Dora Smith, whom I took with me to call upon the Barneses. I just missed him, but found her most cordial, making a great point of my fixing a day to dine there; which I positively declined, though very civilly. I have refused at least thirty invitations to dinner. Then I came home (still with Dora), and found that Mrs. Talfourd *had* dined, and meant me to have some tea! This, however, would not do, so I asked for a devil and a salad, and dressed and ate together, Dora helping. Then William Harness came to settle about our going to Lady Dacre's to-morrow, and to tell me that a servant (he believed Lord Lansdowne's) had been at his house to ask where I was to be found. (I had heard yesterday —I hardly know from whom—that Lord Lansdowne was inquiring about me.) Then came Mrs. Dupuy and William Ogbourn, to go with me to see Malibran. There was an immense house, and a still more immense enthusiasm. And, really, on comparing the matter, I had been deceived about the enthusiasm for *Ion*, for that of to-night was incomparably greater, and the house as full. Malibran is a lovely creature and an incomparable

actress. *She* would be the only person for " Inez " :
and really I should like to write an opera for her.

By-the-way, this new fiddler, Ole Bull, who is
beating Paganini, has taken one of the airs from *our*
opera as the theme of one of his variations in the
concert, which he gives once a week at the King's
Theatre. All the artists say that the plans for the
Houses of Lords and Commons are mere waste of
time ; indeed, no one talks of any of them, except
Barry's, which we have in the *Athenæum*. By-the-
way, that *Athenæum* article is liked, for Talfourd
thinks no praise half enough ; talks still of acting
the part himself at a small theatre ; and would be
capable of buying tickets to fill the house for a week
provided he could in that way keep it going for
that time at Covent Garden. You have no notion
of our poor friend's tremendous inflation. It is
specimen enough to say that he actually expressed
to me great wonder that Lord Lansdowne did not
put off a dinner, which he is to have next Wednesday, and for which tickets have been out these six
weeks, because *Ion* is to be played a second time
that night ! Of me he is furiously jealous ; so he
is of Wordsworth ; but more of me, because people
come to his own house to see me, and walk up to me
and crowd about me whilst he is in the room ; and
most of all is he jealous of Mr. Kenyon, who
(Mrs. Callcott told me) is the most admired and
courted man in town ; and only see how kind he is
to me ! ! I shall ask him to meet me at Chiswick,
and take Wordsworth and Landor.

You can't imagine how well the Duke and I got on. He is a first-rate talker—he *must* be—for I am living in the midst now of all that is best of London conversation, and I have not met with any one who exceeds him: and there was not a moment's pause. I don't think I ever spoke more to my own satisfaction, which is a comfort. He spoke of Captain and Mrs. Gore as very amiable and agreeable. He asked if I knew any Derbyshire persons, which introduced the subject. I told him of Mrs. Forster's geraniums, and he means to go and see them. What a charming person he is ! How I do long to see you and Dash ! Mrs. Gore says you have had a party. This was very foolish, because I am certain I should have managed it much better than you, and I can't imagine what sort of cooking or dinner you would give them. Also I am dying for my Dash and my flowers. I hope the plastering and whitewashing is done ; if not, get it done before I come. I shall certainly come on Friday. Good-bye, my dearest, as I never dare trust any one to put my letters into post except Martha ; they are so often forgotten here.

Ever most faithfully yours,

M. R. Mitford.

To Miss Jephson, Cheltenham

Three Mile Cross, *June* 19, 1836.

I was thinking of writing to you, my dear love, and am very glad to get your address, and to welcome you back to England, which seems a step towards myself. How I wish you were here at this moment! my garden is so exquisite ; your recollection of it can convey nothing like the present beauty or the exquisite colour. It is so changed as to be almost a new thing as to beauty, and yet retaining the old character of close and stage-like scenery, like a back scene " at a play."

I spent ten days in London—ten days crowded with gratification. Wordsworth was there ; I sat next him at dinner three following days, and had the pleasure of finding my old idolatry of the poet turned into a warm affection for the kind, simple, gracious man. We met also almost every morning ; and I saw, on terms of the most agreeable intimacy, Lady Dacre, Lady Morgan, Lady Mary Shepherd, Mrs. Trollope, Mrs. Marcet, Mrs. Callcott, Jane Porter, Joanna Baillie, and I know not how many other females of eminence, to say nothing of all the artists, poets, prosers, talkers, and actors of the day. With the artists I have particular reason to be pleased. Mr. Lucas, whose talent has ripened, and whose portraits this year are amongst the finest in the Exhibition, is coming here to paint my father. I am now come home to work hard, if the people will let me ; for the swarms of visitors and the countless packets of notes and letters which I receive surpass belief. A very clever young artist, Edmund Havell, whose talent in painting animals is really extraordinary, has been (and is) taking a likeness of Dash as large as life. Dash understands the affair, and makes an excellent sitter—very grave and dignified, and a little conscious — peeping stealthily at the portrait, as if afraid of being thought vain if he looked at it too long.

Edwin Landseer has a fine Newfoundland dog, whom he has often painted, and who is content to maintain his posture as long as his master keeps his palette in his hand, however long that may be ; but the moment the palette is laid down, off darts Neptune, and will sit no more that day. Tell Mrs. Price this, if you see her—I mean about Dash's portrait—with my kind love, and that I cannot write yet awhile, being so busy.

You must let me know your whereabouts, and when I am likely to see you. God bless you ! My father's love.

Ever yours,

M. R. Mitford.

To Miss Jephson, Castle Martyr, Ireland

Three Mile Cross, *June* 30, 1837.

So you never heard of the *Pickwick Papers* ! Well ! They publish a number once a month and print 25,000. The bookseller has made about 10,000*l.* by the speculation. It is fun—London life—but without anything unpleasant : a lady might read it all *aloud* ; and it is so graphic, so individual, and so true, that you could curtsey to all the people as you met them in the streets. I did not think there had been a place where English was spoken to which " Boz " had not penetrated. All the boys and girls talk his fun—the boys in the streets ; and yet they who are of the highest taste like it the most.   Sir Benjamin Brodie takes it to read in his carriage between patient and patient ; and Lord Denman studies *Pickwick* on the bench whilst the jury are deliberating.   Do take some means to borrow the *Pickwick Papers*.   It seems like not having heard of Hogarth, whom he resembles greatly, except that he takes a far more cheerful view, a Shakespearian view, of humanity. It is rather fragmentary, except the trial (No. 11 or 12), which is as complete and perfect as any bit of comic writing in the English language.   You must read the *Pickwick Papers*.

My geraniums are splendid this year—magnificent.   We have the whole world to see them.   I wish you were amongst them at this moment ; but we are parching with drought.   Have you read Harriet Martineau's *America* ?   It is a splendid book—ardent, eloquent, earnest, sincere, full of pictures, full of heart.   I do not agree in her theories, but that is another matter.   She is a great honour to her sex and country.   Another book, which is much the fashion, is Mr. Sergeant Talfourd's *Life of Charles Lamb*.   It consists almost wholly of his letters, which are entertaining, although not elegant enough to give me much pleasure.   It is very odd that I should not mind the perfectly low-life of the *Pickwick Papers*, because the closest copies of things that are, and yet dislike the want of elegance in Charles Lamb's letters, which are merely his own fancies ; but I think you will understand the feeling.

If I had time and room I could tell you fifty pretty stories of our young Queen.

Ever most affectionately yours,

M. R. Mitford.

To Miss Barrett, Torquay

Three Mile Cross, *June* 28, 1841.

First, my beloved friend, let me answer your most kind inquiries. I am greatly better. It has been a most remarkable escape ; but a real escape. I cannot yet turn in my bed ; but when up I get about astonishingly well. To say truth, I am, and always have been, a very active person—country-born and country-bred—with great fearlessness and safety of foot and limb. Even *since* this misfortune, Ben having said that half the parish had mounted on a hayrick close by to look at the garden, which lies beneath it (an acre of flowers rich in colour as a painter's palette), I could not resist the sight of the ladder, and one evening when all the men were away, climbed up to take myself a view of my flowery domain. I wish you could see it ! Masses of the Siberian larkspur, and sweet Williams, mostly double, the still brighter new larkspur (*Delphinium Chinensis*), rich as an oriental butterfly—such a size and such a blue ! amongst roses in millions, with the blue and white Canterbury bells (also double),

and the white foxglove, and the variegated monks-
hood, the carmine pea, in its stalwart beauty, the
nemophila, like the sky above its head, the new
erysimum, with its gay orange tufts, hundreds of
lesser annuals, and fuchsias, zinnias, salvias,
geraniums past compt ; so bright are the flowers
that the green really does not predominate amongst
them !

Yes ! I knew you would like those old houses !
Orkwells surpasses in beauty and in preservation
anything I ever saw. Our ancestors were rare
architects. Their painted glass and their carved
oak are unequalled.

Heaven be with you, my dearest !

Ever yours,

M. R. MITFORD.

To Miss Barrett, Wimpole Street

THREE MILE CROSS, March —, 1842.

I have only read the first volume of Madame
D'Arblay's *Diary*. Dr. Johnson appears to the
greatest possible advantage—gentle, tender, kind,
and true ; and Mrs. Thrale—oh, that warm heart !
that lively sweetness ! My old governess knew
her as Mrs. Piozzi, in Wales. She was there as a
governess—neglected, uncared for, as governesses
too often are ; and that sweetest person sought her
out, brought her forward, talked to her, wrote to her,
gave her heart and hope and happiness. There
have been few women who have used riches, and

the station that riches give, so wisely as Mrs. Piozzi.
I used to ask, " Was she happy ? " and the answer
was, " I hope so ; but her animal spirits were so
buoyant—she was so entirely one of those who
become themselves cheered by the effort to cheer
another—that the question is more difficult to
answer than if it concerned one of a temper less
elastic." As to the little Burney, I don't like her
at all, and that 's the truth. A girl of the world—
a woman of the world, for she was twenty-seven
or thereabout—thought clearly and evidently of
nothing on this earth but herself and *Evelina*.

Ever most faithfully yours,

M. R. M.

To Miss Barrett, Wimpole Street

THREE MILE CROSS, *April* 10, 1845.

MINE OWN LOVE,

I have had a wandering poetess here to-day.
She and her mother are driving about the land in
a pony-chaise, selling, for five shillings, books typo-
graphically worth about eightpence — poetically,
good for nothing. The mamma asks one to patron-
ize her daughter — one's " fellow-poetess "— and
won't go till she has got the money. She wanted
to pay *you* a visit, " having heard your name at
Bear Wood." Of course I stopped that, and, as
they are going westward, there is no danger of any
incursion. I gave both ladies some very good
advice, which will very certainly not be taken ; for

such conceit, such ignorance, above all, such total ignorance of the state of literature at this time I never encountered. They asked me for a book to teach the art of poetry—a book of rules, as in arithmetic. For certain, the young lady wants one ; she makes " reign " rhyme to " name " ; " line " to " lime," and so on, and is, by very far, too vain and self-absorbed ever to do better. She has not an atom of the enthusiasm of youth, and admires nobody but herself. But think of the impudence of stopping at the door of everybody, whose name they ever heard, and demanding five shillings, before it is possible to get quit of them ! Their first step was to put their horse in the stable and demand hay and corn. Nothing but pen and ink could inspire such surpassing assurance.

Poor Dr. Baines ! I have been inexpressibly affected by hearing from Mr. Bonomi that, on the very last day of his honoured life, when returning from Bristol, he had said to him, " Now that we are quiet again we will write and ask Miss Mitford to come to Prior Park for a week or ten days." I never saw any man so perfectly interesting, not merely from talent, but from simplicity and goodness. There was a mixture of playfulness and *bonhomie* most enchanting. And he liked me—one always finds out that, and was kinder than I have words to tell. You can hardly imagine, my dearest Emily, how much his death has saddened Bath to me. I had been exceedingly disappointed in the town itself—its deadness and dullness—the cold colour and the monotony of the buildings. Any one accustomed to London must have that feeling ; but Prior Park redeemed all. Did you go there ? Mr. Bonomi is coming to me on his return from his relatives at York ; and I think the establishment will continue. But the guiding spirit is gone. You would have loved Dr. Baines.

There have been, doubtless, difficulties of all sorts during the last unprecedented month of March. Even the violets have been not only late, but scarce ; and yet what enjoyment I have had in getting them !

Ever your own,
M. R. M.

To Charles Boner

I cannot thank you half enough, my dear Mr. Boner, for your most kind and charming letter, and for your good-natured recollection of my wish to possess those spirit-stirring national poems you speak of. I had just met with the " Parisienne " in an earlier edition of Casimir Delavigne's Poems, (rather odd that it should be found in a Brussels collection of 1831, and not in that of '34, is it not ?) so that now my desire is gratified. I find in an account of Béranger (a most delightful one, by-the-by) in the *Critiques et Portraits littéraires* par Sainte-Beuve, that he has published five volumes of Chansons, and when I go to town I shall doubtless be able to pick them out of the contents of Rolandi's library, whose catalogue with its seven supplements would be a puzzle much harder than that of the Sphinx. Thank you too, for telling me of *Les Petits Manèges d'une Femme vertueuse*—that will be by Balzac ? *Les Paysans* I have seen, at least the first volume, and I don't choose to believe it a true representation, because I do not believe that the mass of a great nation can be so base and cunning ; though I admit that the Marquis de Custine, in his very clever work, *Le Monde comme il est*, gives pretty nearly the same account of the peasantry of Normandy. But Balzac must be a cockney Parisian (if such an idiom may be allowed). The boudoir or the opera are his proper scenes, and he has no love for the people, which is not only a great fault, but a great mistake in these days, when they are rising in importance every hour. Georges Sand and Eugène Sue are wiser, as well as the great old Bard ; and they will have their reward not only in the diffusion of their reputation, but in its duration. Even Mrs. Gore, who may be looked on as a sort of weather-cock to show which way the wind of popularity blows, has just put forth a Christmas Story, in which the scene is laid in a farm house, and the squire's son marries a clerk's daughter.

Before I forget, let me tell you that on consulting all the military authorities within reach (one of them a drill sergeant), I find them unanimous in deciding that the attitude in question corresponds to the word " Carry arms "—it is in fact the position

of a sentinel on duty.   With regard to the " Sand-
man," we have no such personage among our
nursery bugbears, and it would not be understood
without an explanatory note, and even then would
be a bit of foreign idiom unworthy of your truly
English translation.   The word that may be ac-
counted synonymous amongst us as a threat to
naughty children is " Old Bogie."   On this point
I have inquired of nurses and governesses and
children themselves (a Yorkshire dame and a
damsel from Cornwall were among the cate-
chumens), and the universal response was " Old
Bogie," though who the gentleman so designated
may be is more than I can venture to guess.   But
I think you will be quite safe in putting his name
in the front of your story.   I look forward with
great interest to the publication of that charming
book, which I shall enjoy quite as much as if I were
one of your legitimate readers of eight years old,
instead of fifty-eight next Tuesday.   Is the other
translation the History of Rudolf of Hapsburg ? or
have I, with my customary infelicity, made a
mistake in the Emperor's name ?   Do be so good
as to tell it me, and don't be discouraged by the
irksomeness of translation.   You will find rendering
poetry more a work of art, and therefore more
self-rewarding.

I wish I had any news to send you, but I hear
from town of little except the amateur play—(Ben
Jonson's *Every Man in his Humour*) in which
Messrs. Dickens, and Forster, of the *Examiner*, and

Mark Lemon and Douglas Jerrold, have been figuring. They say that Mr. Forster's " Kitely " was excellent ; and one new paper, ultra-whig, is coming forth with the name of Mr. Dickens, who is to write the *Feuilletons*, and the combined aid of all the *Punch* people. It is thought a great risk.

The most important book has been Carlyle's *Cromwell*, in which the mutual jargon of the biographer and his subject is very curious. Never was such English seen. The Lord Protector comes much nearer to speaking plain than his historian. I have been reading with great interest (thinking of you) Leslie's *Life of Constable* ; a charming book about an admirable man. Heaven bless you ! dear Mr. Boner. I wonder whether an English direction will find you. Forgive all faults, and believe me ever most faithfully yours,

MARY RUSSELL MITFORD.

To Charles Boner

THREE MILE CROSS, *April*, 1846.

I thank you heartily, my dear sir, for your very interesting letter, and shall look forward with no common expectation to a translation carefully made by one so very competent. In these days, when translating, composition, all sorts of book-work seem done as if by steam, it is something choice and rare to find poet and publisher agreeing to recognize the virtue of slowness. Well, the trees of long growth are those of long life ; the gourd of the night withers before sunset, so it will be seen with these pen-and-ink plants, be sure.

I yesterday received from Miss Barrett a very interesting letter sent to her by Miss Martineau. She will get into her cottage before April, and gives a charming account of her terrace, her field, and her quarry, whence she got the stones for her terrace wall, and which she means to hang with ivies and honeysuckles, and tuft with foxgloves and ferns. She gives also a charming account of the great Poet, although he has just lost his only brother, and had bad news from his sick daughter-in-law.

I had had an excellent account of him a few days ago from our mutual friend, Henry Crabbe Robinson (also the bosom friend of Goethe), who had been spending a month at Ambleside, to be near him. He says that his great resource is whist—the great resource of age. Somebody comes to see him and brings two packs of cards, which last till the same somebody comes again the following year. Mr. Robinson said that Miss Martineau was much in favour, not only with Mr. Wordsworth, but with his female coterie, Mrs. Fletcher, Miss Fenwick, Mrs. Arnold, and Mrs. Wordsworth, quite a flower-garden of ladies such as Richardson used to cultivate. If I were there I should want *men* (at fifty-eight one may say so, and you will know what I mean : an infusion of manly intellect and manly spirit is indispensable in a country life). Henry Chorley passed two days with me last week : he says that Mr. Reeve is in Paris. His little girl runs about *his* house (I mean Henry Chorley's) like a pet kitten, and is, he says, a most sweet little creature. I hope that Mr. Chorley's play will be brought out at Covent Garden by Miss Cushman, who is now, to my great horror, playing Romeo to her sister's Juliet. I don't like she-Romeos, but she has made what is called a hit, though hardly, I should think, of the best sort. How can a woman make the right sensation in doublet and hose !

Is not Hood a great serious poet ? Are not the " Bridge of Sighs " and the " Haunted House " magnificent ? Henry Russell has been setting and singing the " Song of the Shirt," and being a great tragic actor (in spite of the music), it is a very fine thing. I agree heartily with you about Mr. Proctor's songs. They come next to Burns's, I think, and far before Moore's. You will be glad to hear that he has just got a commissionership, and is released from the drudgery of conveyancing. His wife (Basil Montague's wife's daughter) is a very pleasant person.

I am going to Paris in May, dear Mr. Boner. Can you help me to any letters of introduction ; not to grand people, of course, but to such as you would like to see yourself ? The man whom I should best like to know is, I am afraid, not seeable—Béranger. Think of this, dear friend. A very clever and very excellent young man is to escort me, and probably a young lady, and, being artistic, he would like to know any actor or musician. I think to spend six weeks there. Miss Barrett and Mr. Kenyon say that I shall not go, which, if I wanted a motive to keep my resolution, would of course supply one. Miss Barrett is so much better that she sits up in an arm-chair, and walks across the room, although she does not leave it.   Can you help her and me to any titles of French novels ? Any of Balzac's or Charles de Bernard ?   Adieu, my dear Mr. Boner.

Ever most faithfully yours,

M. R. M.

To Charles Boner

THREE MILE CROSS, *Sept.*, 1846.

I have to thank you, dear Mr. Boner, for your most kind letter, and for your verses, which are full of power ; and now you must summon all your indulgence and all your faith in the sincerity of my esteem and my good will, and allow me to entreat you to find some better literary agent than my poor self.   I live in the country, going rarely, if ever, to London, and then to one house only.   I have as few literary friends and acquaintances as is well possible, and of the race of Editors and Journalists I know absolutely nothing.   Then if I write to proprietors of magazines, or newspapers, or periodicals of any sort, requesting them to insert a friend's poem, the reply is sure to be that they overflow with poetry, but that they want a prose story from me, and most likely they trump up a story of some previous application, and *dun* with as much authority as if I really owed them the article, and they had paid for it.

Now all this is not only supremely disagreeable to me, but makes me a most ineffective and useless mediator for you.

You should have a man upon the spot for those things, and not an old woman at a distance, hating the trade of authorship, and keeping as much aloof as possible from all its *tracasseries*. You will understand from this, my good friend, that if I were to write a story for a book of yours, I should have half-a-dozen people claiming some imaginary promise, and clamouring, as if I had robbed them in giving away a worthless tale. As to the *Times*, I am, it is true, intimate with the proprietors, but it happens that Bear Wood is the only house in England where that universal paper is never mentioned, or, if mentioned, only to be denied. So, my dear friend, you must establish, when you come to England again, some correspondence with one or other of the thousand and one literary people in London—which I am sure you can do most easily.

The great news of the season is the marriage of my beloved friend, Elizabeth Barrett, to Robert Browning. Do you know him ? I have seen him once only, many years ago. He is, I hear, from all quarters, a man of immense attainment and great conversational power. As a poet, I think him over-rated. The few things of his which are clear, seem to me as weak as water ; and those on which his reputation rests, *Paracelsus*, and *Bells and Pomegranates*, are to me as so many riddles. I dread exceedingly for her the dreadful trial of the journey across France to Italy, and the total change of life and habits. Mrs. Jameson and her niece joined them at Paris, but my last letter was from Moulins, and she then seemed much exhausted. God grant she be not quite worn out by that terrible journey to Pisa ! The prettiest account of a love-match for a long while is to be found in the sixth volume of *Madame D'Arblay's Memoirs*, excellently arranged by my friend Henry Chorley. It is charming to see the account of their cottage life—she working for him in England, he for her in France. I have also been much amused by the *Coq du Clocher*, by the author who calls himself Jerome Paturot. Do you know anything about him ? He is immensely clever, and very entertaining.

Tell me anything about French literature—I know little of German, and, to say the truth, take small interest in it, though Count Pocci interests me much from his universality of talent. Good bye, my dear Mr. Boner. Don't be angry with me, but believe me ever very faithfully yours,

M. R. MITFORD.

To Charles Boner

THREE MILE CROSS, *Dec.* 16, 1847.

I write to you on my birthday, dearest Mr. Boner, the day that seems to gather one nearer to those whom one loves and values ; and I send you all the good wishes that I know you would pour forth on your poor old friend on this her sixtieth birthday,

if you did but know it. I hope and trust that you
are better in Germany than we are in England.
Influenza is in every house quite as a pestilence ;
illness of every sort besides. For my own part I
have been suffering all the autumn. But besides
this, I have had a great affliction in the death of my
dear old dog. You remember him, I am sure, with
his bright auburn curls, dark and shining as the
rind of the horse-chestnut, and the golden light
that played over them in the sunbeams ! I am
sure you remember my poor pretty favourite. But
nothing but my long experience of his high qualities
can convey a notion of his real value ; his sweetness,
his gentleness, his affection, his over-estimate of
kindness, his forgetfulness of wrong, his recollection
of old friends, old servants, were most remarkable.

At the end of three years he suddenly recognized
a friend of mine who had been good to him, jumped
upon her, and even licked her hands and feet.
He never forgot any one who had been kind to him.
I cannot tell you how I miss him, and his sagacity
was such as to make him really a companion ; his
sagacity and his sympathy—for that, I suppose,
was the real charm after all—the loving where I
loved. If you remember, he recognized you last
year. The only alleviation to our loss is, that he
died without pain, and without any of the infirmi-
ties of age, which if he had lived much longer he
would, I fear, have suffered, for he was thirteen
or fourteen years old.

I have been thinking of you and talking of you

lately, having been engaged (as indeed I still am) in making out a list of secular books for lending libraries for the poor. The young wife of a clergy- man, a girl of sense, wrote to me to say she could find no such list except of tracts and sermons ! so dear Mr. Lovejoy and I have fallen to work, and when we have completed our labour we shall send you a copy. We mean to set down the very best books (which are luckily the cheapest), upon the plan of Napoleon, who you remember in throwing open the theatres of Paris after a victory or a marriage, always chose a play of Corneille, or of Molière, and always found his choice justified by the gratification and intelligence of the audience.

Just as we were thinking of this subject William Chambers, of Edinburgh, came to pay me a visit, and has assisted us by a good deal of information and advice, such as getting parishes to agree and interchange their libraries. He says that the obstacles to all education in England and Scotland, are the clergy. I am quite of that mind from my own experience, but I did not expect to hear him say so. He is a very superior person. He has persuaded Miss Edgeworth to write a book for young people—remarkable considering her age, for she must be turned of eighty, but still one that justifies my theory of not writing too long, inasmuch as it reads just like an imitation of her own better works. It is called *Orlandino*, and is a story of a lad reformed from drinking by a younger lad.

Alfred Tennyson's poem, *The Princess, A Medley*,

is at last announced to be published in a few days :
I am very anxious to see it. Thank you for your
list, dear friend. I mean your French list. I am
now reading M. de Baranté's great book on the
Dukes of Burgundy. Very captivating historians,
are these modern French writers, full of picture
and colour, interesting you in the story of the
country they write about, but whether (I am
especially thinking of Lamartine now) they may
give a very correct idea of the people, is doubtful.
Lamartine has a wonderful tendency to make his
people better, so that one wonders (the crimes
having certainly been committed) who, according
to him, was to blame.

Is Eugène Sue writing now ? I have seen
nothing of his since *Martin*, and one cannot afford
to lose the creator of Rigolette. Your books are
still at Windsor Castle ; Miss Skerrett—herself an
excellent Danish as well as German scholar—
praises the translation greatly. Messrs. Grant and
Griffith have just sent me your new volume of
Andersen. Thank you for it. Heaven bless you,
my dear friend.

To Charles Boner

THREE MILE CROSS, *Sept.*, 1848.

John Ruskin, the Oxford Graduate, is a very
elegant and distinguished-looking young man, tall,
fair, and slender—too slender, for there is a consumptive look, and I fear a consumptive tendency

—the only cause of grief that he has ever given to his parents. He must be, I suppose, twenty-six or twenty-seven, but he looks much younger, and has a gentle playfulness—a sort of pretty waywardness, that is quite charming.

He took a fancy to my writings as you did, dearest friend, and came to see me by the introduction of our dear friend Mrs. Cockburn (the Mary Duff of Lord Byron), and now we write to each other, and I hope love each other as you and I do. He passed a fortnight at Keswick, but did not see Wordsworth, although Wordsworth and he had often met in London. The family did not seem to wish it, he said, and in short both he and I feared that there must have been some truth in reports about the decline of intellect of the Bard of Rydal Mount. Nevertheless, Mr. Sergeant Talfourd has just dedicated to him his *Final Memorials of Charles Lamb*. Two volumes of letters, containing such as could not, for the tragedy they tell, be published until the death of Miss Lamb, and of others which, for a contrary reason—their comedy—were necessarily suppressed until poor simple George Dyer was safe under ground. Nothing can be better than Lamb's share of these volumes. I can't say so much for the Sergeant's. Bulwer has published a novel (*Harold, the last Saxon King*), very dull as a tale, but good as history, doing justice *to* Harold and *on* William. By-the-way, William Smith, of the Inner Temple, sent me the other day a volume of tragedies, one of which, " Athelwold," is very fine. Do you know him ? I never heard the name before. Now that there is an end of the acted drama, people are writing fine plays.

Mr. Kingsley (almost a neighbour of mine) has just written a very fine dramatic poem on the story of Elizabeth of Hungary, called the *Saint's Tragedy* ; and another neighbour, whose father and mother I know well, has just written the Oxford prize poem, " Columbus in Chains." It is very elegant, and I rejoice at it, for all their sakes. His father, the Rev. C. Blackstone, was a friend and correspondent of Dr. Arnold. The author of *Jane Eyre* (believed to be a governess, and to have been brought up at the establishment of Carus Wilson) has published another novel. And now, dear friend, it is time that I should release you from this tremendous letter. Heaven bless you. Send me word that you are quite well.

Ever yours,

M. R. M.

To Charles Boner

THREE MILE CROSS, *April* 2, 1849.

Thank you a thousand and a thousand times, my very dear friend, for your great goodness. May I keep the letter you were so very kind as to send me till the autumn ? Because it now seems likely that my journey may be postponed till then.

I am just in the discomfort of changing servants, not my own dear little maid who waits upon me and walks with me, and is literally and really my right hand, but the younger girl who does the housework, and every now and then grows out of her place and wants promotion and higher wages. This has happened now, and it will not do to let an untried stranger have charge of my poor cottage, until we have had some experience of the new damsel, who is to come to us at Easter, and whom we chose out of three sisters because she sate at work with a little baby brother on her knee, and had tidy hair and a nice bright and good-natured face. What details to send to one who lives in a palace, and hears the turret clock strike at midnight while the watchman traverses the great corridors! But some day you may have just such a little poetical cottage establishment of your own. I believe you would be very happy in such an one, although, I can't tell why, but I always think that your story will end like a romance, by your marrying some great lady and having a château to your own share. Such things do happen now and then in life as well as in books, and you are just the sort of person to justify such a choice and do honour to such a destiny.

I have heard twice of Mrs. Browning since I wrote to you, the first letter to tell me that she was safely confined with a fine boy; the second, that the mother and infant were going on well. The first letter is the only one I ever received from Mr. Browning.

So you are reading Lucas Montigny's *Life of*

Mirabeau. I am sure it will interest you above all things—it did me. I got only the first three volumes from Rolandi's, and I could not wait for a parcel from London, but sent about the neighbourhood till I met with a friend who had the book, and who sent me twenty-one other volumes of and about Mirabeau. Amongst these were three other biographies—Dumont's lying book, the *Lettres de Cachet*, the *Histoire Secrète de la Cour de Berlin*, and three very thick volumes of *Discours*, containing all his speeches in the National Assembly. I have also read the two trials with his own memoirs and speeches there, and almost all that he ever wrote, except two or three books that never should have been printed, and the famous *Lettres originales du Donjon de Vincennes*, the celebrated letters to Sophie, of which many of the biographies contain long extracts, and which I must read altogether.

The extracts from those letters seem to me as far superior to Rousseau, as passion is to sentiment, or truth to fiction. I must have those five volumes. Lucas Montigny is somewhat of a prig, and does not half enough envy, hate, and detest the Marquis and le Bailli ; but I go along with him quite in his enthusiasm for that great man his father, whose faults seem to have been mainly produced by the tremendous tyranny of which he was the object. The domestic tyrannies, his family, the crown, the laws of the kingdom—the provincial parliament— all these, acting upon his burning southern temperament and his tempestuous passions, combined to

form that stormy youth ; but with all his faults of
conduct, how great and how wise a man he was !
How much before his age ! What a definition of
free trade did he give in the brief phrase *laisser faire*
and *laisser passer* ! What a picture of the French
public when he said that for them there were no
such words as *toujours* or *jamais* ! How genial he
was, how kind, how generous, how lovable, how
loving ! One of his biographers gives a vivid
account of the connection of the Marquis with the
woman de Pailly, who had been a *femme de chambre*
and who ruled them all ; and *he* to dare to blame
the disorders into which his own avarice and
tyranny, and his cold-hearted daughter-in-law drove
her gifted husband ! Does not that unworthy
woman resemble Marie Louise ? Mirabeau might
well say that his flight was too high and too unequal
for her.

In one of the memoirs not inserted in Lucas
Montigny, he blames himself " for expecting fruit
from a tree that could only bear flowers." Is not
this most beautiful in its indulgence and its grace ?
and how like Napoleon's forbearance to Marie
Louise ! Do tell me all you think of Mirabeau,
and do get the *Discours*. They are magnificent.

I have been reading *Les Confidences*, a pretty
book which, whether true or not (and to me,
especially coming after the realities of Mirabeau, it
bears falsehood stamped upon every page), gives
one the very worst possible idea of the writer.
This pleased me most : next to the having an

enthusiasm justified, one likes to find oneself borne out in a prejudice. He is jealous of Napoleon's fame, as all vain men are—as Lord Byron was. But just fancy what Napoleon would have done in his position last February—or Mirabeau. They were men of thought and action, Lamartine is merely a man of words. Just (to exemplify his falseness) watch the dates in *Les Confidences*. You will find him fifteen when he makes love in 1805, and twenty in 1815. Indeed twenty is his favourite age. He sticks at that, just as the maid who is about to leave me called herself nineteen when she came to me two years ago, and calls herself nineteen still. It is clear that the Raphael story is to dovetail in with the end of *Les Confidences* which (in the edition I have seen—is there any continuation ?) leaves him on the road to Aix, and to another tragedy. Only fancy a man of sixty writing all this rubbish about girls dying for love of him—a man who is an historian and an orator, and who pretends to be a statesman ! Think whether Napoleon or Mirabeau would have done so. The Sophie correspondence came out after the great writer's death, and without his suspecting that it ever would appear.

I have only read the first part of *Chateaubriand*. It is interesting, and seems perfectly true. Talk to me of your impressions of Mirabeau and of these books, and of any new French ones, and tell me what you hear of Louis Napoleon. I have not room here for a pretty story about him that my friend Mr. Hinton told me. He was much beloved

and respected at Leamington, where he lived for a
year. Above all, dear friend, tell me of yourself.
Poor Hartley Coleridge ! How the great names
go out !

Ever yours,

M. R. M.

P.S.—I am reading another collection of Horace
Walpole.

To Charles Boner

THREE MILE CROSS, *May* 6, 1849.

If I wanted anything beyond my own regard for
you, dearest Mr. Boner, and your own most kind
letters, I should be reminded of you by the nightingales which are just now singing in such abun-
dance, and peopling all the woods and fields with
the notes that you have described so well. We
have one most exquisite bird in my poor garden.
Oh, such a bird ! Did you ever remark how much
nightingale differs from nightingale in force and
power and sweetness and variety ? I have often
noticed it, but never so much as this year, when *our*
bird, as K. proudly calls it, and one of equal quality,
about two miles off, seem to me to excel all their
compeers as much as the greatest singer of the
Opera beats his inferiors of the Chorus. Now
surely this is not the case with other feathered
songsters. Blackbird does not differ from blackbird, nor thrush from thrush. K. and I agreeing
perfectly in the superiority of the *two*, dispute as

to their separate merits, I rather preferring the distant singer, whom I go to hear every night, she fighting stoutly for *our* neighbour of the garden, as I believe, because it is ours ; such is the magic of the possessive pronoun, even when the application be a mere fiction, as our beloved bird will indicate when he and his mate have reared their family, and they all fly away.   All happiness go with them !   I love those birds as if they were conscious of my gratitude and affection ; and really, I half think that my pet, the far-off neighbour, does know my love for him, for he never fails to salute me as often as I draw near.

How very kind your German and French friends are to me : I owe it chiefly, of course, to your partiality, dearest friend, to which I am but too proud to owe all manner of benefits, but yet I have been accustomed to feel grateful for the good opinion of German readers of English books.   It is astonishing how well they know our literature, and how little, to judge from French writers, our authors are known in France.   The only one whom they appear really to appreciate is Mrs. Radcliffe— Anne Radcliffe, as they call her, for they do not even mis-spell her name.   It is quite amusing to see how much a writer, well nigh forgotten in England, is admired in France.   I dare say, now, you never read a page of her novels, and yet such critics as Sainte-Beuve, such poets as Victor Hugo, such novel- ists as Balzac and Georges Sand, to say nothing of a thousand inferior writers, talk of her in raptures.

I will venture to say that she is quoted fifty times where Scott is quoted once.   Indeed, I believe that the *real* merits both of Scott and Shakespeare are little known to them, although they may know the stories of both from operas and so forth, as the mob of the English (by-the-way) know Beaumarchais' great comedies.   I used to think that Shakespeare could not be at all rendered in French, but Alfred de Vigny has made a very fair translation of *Othello*, and Madame Tastu has executed the more difficult task of transposing the garden scene of *Romeo and Juliet* into verse that is really high poetry.

When you thank your fair friend for her goodness to me, tell her that I still hope to deliver her letter. Perhaps in the autumn, for Paris will be too hot for me now, although the weather here is very cold and stormy.   The hail the other day swept every chimney in the house, and did much mischief to gardens and fields.   Henry Chorley says that I had no loss in not meeting him in Paris, for that he never felt so strongly the miserable hollowness and trustlessness of the French character under the thinnest possible crust of gaiety.   Well, I hope better things.   I like their literature with all its faults, and am well disposed to like them.   Tell me if, with all his faults, Mirabeau is not adorable, and yet you ought to read his *Discours* and his *Mémoires pour Consulter*, and a great deal besides, that good M. Lucas Montigny would not put into his book, because, forsooth, it had been printed before.   He is a sad prig, and yet I should like to

know him, too, for the sake of the great man whom
he has written about.

Good night! dear friend. I wish I were likely
to see you this summer, but I fear there is no such
good luck in store. Our poor little boy—K.'s little
boy—has been very ill, but he is now, thank God,
doing well.

Ever most faithfully yours,

MARY RUSSELL MITFORD.

To Charles Boner

THREE MILE CROSS, April 7, 1850.

I cannot tell you, dear friend, how glad I was to
get your letter, and to find that you had received
mine. My good opinion of the book (*Chamois
Hunting*) has gone on increasing. Don't alter it
at all. Don't change the style; it gives to it
individuality and identity, and really it is graceful
and pretty, and the whole book will be charming.
I have read almost all that Carlyle has written, and
was like you much struck with his *Hero Worship*.
I am afraid, however, I do not like him quite as
well as you do. In the first place I have a firm
persuasion that clear thoughts make clear words,
and that where great obscurity exists in the language,
the fault will generally be found lower and deeper.
In the next I detest and abhor certain atrocities
and abominations, which I suppose he means for
humour, and which abound especially in the two
huge volumes about Cromwell. Thirdly, I mis-

trust his sincerity and earnestness, chiefly because he says one thing on Monday and another on Tuesday, contradicting himself with as little scruple as he contradicts other people.

I am told by his admirers that the *French Revolution* is his great work. Perhaps it may be, only I am quite convinced that nobody who did not know the story previously would gain the slightest idea of it from Mr. Carlyle's three volumes, and that is not my theory of a history. His last work, which I have not seen, is said to be eminently socialist, but until translated into English I would always give him the benefit of a doubt. For the rest he has a large following, and is so glad to increase it that you would be received with open arms. Of poetry he is intolerant—at least two friends of mine, Elizabeth Barrett and Mr. Bennett, each sent him a present of their works, and received answers so nearly alike (I saw both of them), that it seemed to me a set form, kept for the purpose. He praised the powers of both lady and gentleman, but deprecated the use made of them, and advised both parties " to say rather than to sing," which advice being construed, meant, I suppose, to take to prose instead of verse.

The counsel lost him both his admirers. I have never heard either of them mention his name since. For my own part I never saw him, and having never had any sort of intercourse with him, am at least free from personal prejudice. Do you know Emerson, the American Essayist ? It seems to me that he would have been a great writer and thinker, if Carlyle had not fallen in his way. Now he appears a mere copyist of the Scotchman. At one time I apprehended his queer jargon to be German idiom (I mean Carlyle's), although his *Life of Schiller* comes nearer to English than his later works, but a German Jewess, who was talking to me about him, said, he was the most difficult English author that she had ever attempted to translate into German.

After you have read more of him, you will like him less. I am quite sure that your fine taste will be repelled by the horrible coarseness of some of his nicknames in the Cromwell book. He is constantly talking of flunkeyism, and trades upon half-a-dozen cant words of that order.

Oh how I should have liked to see that mask of Napoleon! His face is the very ideal of beauty in all the prints and paintings : the upper part all power, the lower all sweetness. The greatest sin ever committed by a nation was ours in letting that great man perish at St. Helena.

I have just finished the third volume of Southey's *Life and Letters* : all his old friends complain of the selection and the omissions, and say that Cuthbert Southey, the son, who is editing the work, is a young man quite incompetent to choose from the enormous mass of correspondence at his disposal. I only hope that all will be eventually published, for although there is much in which I do not agree, I delight in the letters and could read a hundred such.

How very glad I shall be to see you ! You must

be here as much as you can.   Perhaps I shall be in
town part of the time.   The more I think of the
stag part the less I think any change will be needed.
I like the book more and more.

This is my last word.

Ever yours,

MARY RUSSELL MITFORD.

To Mrs. Jennings, Portland Place

SWALLOWFIELD, *Dec.* 31, 1850.

How glad I am to see your dear handwriting again,
dearest Mrs. Jennings, and how much more glad
should I be to see yourself !   It was a great temptation that which Mrs. Dupuy put in my way, to
come to town and go with her to your house on
Christmas day.   I do quite understand your feelings.   A father (and such a father) is a loss never to
be replaced ; but there is comfort and satisfaction
in such a recollection ; and even your children
will be the better, ay ! much the better, for having
to look back to such a grandfather, linked to them
by such parents.   So out of grief springs hope.

Mr. Kingsley took me quite by surprise in his
extraordinary fascination.   I have never seen a
man of letters the least like him, for, in general,
the *beau idéal* of a young poet remains a *beau idéal*.
They are mostly middle-aged (sometimes elderly),
conceited, affected, foppish, vulgar.   Mr. Kingsley
is not only a high-bred gentleman, but has the most
charming admixture of softness and gentleness,

with spirit, manliness, and frankness—a frankness quite transparent—and a cordiality and courtesy that would win any heart. He did win his own sweet wife entirely by this charm of character. She was a girl of family, fortune, fashion, and beauty ; he a young curate, without distinction of any sort— without even literary distinction, for he had not then published. He loved her—she loved him ; and, without any unseemly elopement, they lived down and loved down a pretty strong family opposition, and were married. Since that, Sir John Cope gave him the living of Eversley ; and he has won a very high fame, and the love of all his parish and all his neighbourhood. He is quite young ; and though, I suppose, he does not generally intend to go fox-hunting, yet it sometimes happens that his horse carries him into the midst of the chase, when he is always in at the death, eager and delighted as a boy. I cannot tell you how much I like him. Miss Bremer was at his house, just before we became acquainted, and he was much pleased with her. She stayed too short a time, or we should have met. He is now engaged upon a work (in *Fraser*) treating of Alexandria in the fifth century—a sort of story like Lockhart's *Valerius* or Mr. Ware's *Palmyra*—but he is greatest as a poet. I know nothing more touching than that song in *Alton Locke*.

I am charmed with my new cottage. The scenery is delightful, and the neighbours most kind and pleasant. Perhaps, when the days get long and the weather fine, you will come and see me—

won't you ? I do hope to get to town in time to
see you this year. You know that my last visit
was regulated by the arrival of Mrs. Browning.

Yours, attached and affectionate,

M. R. MITFORD.

To Charles Boner

SWALLOWFIELD, *July* 20, 1851.

I do not know, dear Mr. Boner, whether, when I
last wrote, I was as dismally lame as I am now, or
rather, whether the lameness had lasted so long as
to become a settled infirmity. I rather crawl than
walk, and am put down in the green lane at three
or four o'clock with my little maid and my little
dog and my camp stool, and fetched again at seven
or eight o'clock, that I may have the air without
fatigue.

Partly this lameness, partly the absence of
curiosity, have kept me in the country. Chairs
are only admitted for an hour or two to the Great
Exhibition early on the Saturday morning, and as
Mrs. Browning has advanced as far as Paris towards
London, I wait to know whether she really does
mean to come to England this year before making
up my mind to take the journey without the chance
of seeing her. Unless she comes, I don't think I
shall get to London. I dread the fatigue, and the
crowd, and the excitement, and have really less
desire to go than can well be conceived. I never

was a sight-seer, and the more one questions people
about this the less one finds oneself attracted.   Sam,
whom I sent, says that one-third of the stalls consists of stockings and calico, and things as common
as that, and it is wonderful how people are cooling
towards it.   We always were a nation of idolaters :
always avenging ourselves upon our poor idols for
our own idolatry.   We make gods of wood and
stone, and then we knock them to pieces, as many a
poet, first over-rated then under-rated, can testify,
and so we shall do by this, although, to do the most
sensible people whom I know justice, they have
always laughed at the fashionable madness.   Taken
at the very best, it is furniture, not art, and if it
come to be a winter garden, will probably look
better when clothed with gorgeous creepers and
filled with fountains, and statues, and flowering
shrubs, than it does now.

Mrs. Browning sent me her book.   It is a dull
tirade on Italian politics.   When I say dull and yet
vigorously written, that sounds like a contradiction,
but it is not so.   The subject, which is not largely
though forcibly treated, is so unreal that it excites
no sympathy, for it seems to me out of the question
that a people without recent poetry, without living
literature, without even an attempt at eloquence—
whose last great writer was Alfieri, whose sculpture
has dwindled into wood-carving, whose pictorial
art into mosaic copies, who have not even produced
one man of mark in this general tossing up of nations,
—should be ripe for freedom and self-government.

Year by year they seem to me dwindling. Even
music, which held by them longest, is now dying
away. They have still singers, but they have no
composers. Italy is an extinct volcano. The very
smoke is gone, and it seems to me wrong as well as
foolish to try to provoke a struggle, which can only
end in the reaction always so fatal to progress and
rational liberty. Don't you agree with me ? There
are one or two tolerable passages, but the metre is
harsh and unattractive, and the triple rhyme of
Dante quite unsuited to English verse ; and the
only result of the book will be a bill at Chapman
and Hall's, and a total exclusion from Italy for the
writer in case she wants to return thither. It will
make no hit here.

The *Stones of Venice* has a great success. The
illustrations by the author are exquisite, and the
writing, as always, is good, with his characteristic
faults, which people almost accept for beauties.
Hawthorne's *House with the Seven Gables* is even
finer in the same way than *The Scarlet Letter*—
the legendary part dim, shadowy, and impressive,
and the living characters exquisitely true, vivid, and
healthful. The heroine, Phoebe, is almost a Shakespearian creation, as fresh and charming as the
Rigolette of Eugène Sue. You and the Princess
are very good in liking my poor articles ; and as to
the *Lady's Companion*, your knowledge of it is
later than mine. I think the last proof I corrected
was one of Fishing Songs. God bless you.

To Miss Russell

SWALLOWFIELD, *April* 29, 1852.

Do not, I beseech you, think me impertinent in intruding upon a grief so sacred and so sweet. I know that you and dear Lady Russell need no assurance of my sympathy ; and yet I cannot feel satisfied without saying how deeply I join with all who knew him in lamenting the death of the great and good man who has just been summoned to a happier world, leaving to his children that of which even death cannot bereave them—the rich inheritance of his reputation and his example.

Besides the eminent public services recognized by races so various, and acknowledged by parties who agree in little else, the private character of Sir Henry Russell always seemed to me to unite in the happiest combination those qualities which command admiration, affection, and respect. His rare accomplishments, his extensive and accurate knowledge, his great conversational power, the charm of his manner, or rather, of that unfailing benevolence which manner only imitates, rendered him the most interesting and delightful of companions. An exquisite judge and keen lover of literature, he joined the fervent application of youth to the bland indulgence of age, and, loving the highest best, was tolerant of every style so that it were distinguished by purity and truth.

Of what he was in his nearer and dearer connec-

tions, of his constancy in friendship, his excellence
as a master and a landlord, as brother, husband,
and father, the regrets of those whom he has left
behind speak eloquently, and will speak long.
And yet, dearest Miss Russell, the very virtues
which now add to your sorrow will, as that sorrow
melts into tender recollection, become the sweet
sources of comfort to those who love him best.

Do not trouble yourself to write, only send me
word how you all are. I trust that the rain will
bring with it milder winds, and restore you to the
genial influences of Nature—ever a consoler to
those who love her, as you do—and to your accustomed walks amongst the spring flowers and the
budding trees.

To the Rev. William Harness, Kensington Gore

Swallowfield, *Nov.* 10, 1852.

Thank you a thousand times, dear friend, for your
most kind and tempting invitation ; but although
much better, I cannot help feeling that a very little
exertion and excitement would overset me.

I have heard often from M—— S—— lately, and
I know no part of her letters that gave me greater
pleasure than when, speaking of Windsor Castle,
she said, " and with seven children, there is at least
plenty of noise " ; it sounded quite homely and
hearty, for a palace.

The people are crazy about *Uncle Tom's Cabin.*
I read about a hundred pages, and found the book

so painful, that I put it down, and certainly am not likely to take it up again. It is one-sided, exaggerated, false—with some cleverness, but of a very disagreeable kind. Nevertheless, if there had been the great literary merit they talk of I think I should have gone on. My belief is, that the *de*-merits of the book have more to do with its popularity than any sort of excellence ; the cant about slavery being a good cry—such as we English love to get up on certain subjects—against the Emperors, for instance, uncle and nephew, or against the Pope. After all, how little has this sort of immediate popularity to do with lasting reputation ! Look at the great novelists of the day, Dickens and Thackeray (although it is some injustice to Thackeray to class them together, for he can write good English when he chooses, and produce a striking and consistent character) ; but look at their books, so thoroughly false and unhealthy in different ways ; Thackeray's so world-stained and so cynical, Dickens's so meretricious in sentiment and so full of caricature. Compare them with Scott and Miss Austen, and then say if they can live. Neither of them can produce an intelligent, right-minded, straightforward woman, such as one sees every day ; and a love story from Thackeray could hardly fail to be an abomination.

Have you read Mr. Kingsley's *Phaeton* ?   A dialogue in the manner of Plato—or rather a dialogue within a dialogue. There is the usual inconclusiveness ; but yet one gathers much good ;

warnings not to let the love of nature degenerate
into an exclusive worship, to the neglect of the
Creator ; and injunctions to seek the faith of the
Low Church, without the narrowness. Perhaps
I like this pamphlet the better because I so entirely
like the author. He spent one of these wet mornings with me, and is certainly one of the most
charming persons in the world. You must meet.
He was so sorry to have missed you ! He is not a
bit like an author—only a frank, charming, genial
young man. Then I have had all manner of
visitors spending the day here ; Bayard Taylor,
the American traveller, Agnes Niven and Miss
Denman. By-the-way Miss Denman has the
ladies' college mania ! The more I hear of it, the
more I dislike it.—I shall do nothing for it.—I
should not, even if I did not wish to help the
dear Russells with the Swallowfield schools.—The
college being a device for the promotion of governesses, of whom, poor things, there are already
too many.

Poor Daniel Webster ! Mr. Fields wrote to me
whilst the mourning guns were booming over the
harbour. He says that, never since Washington,
has America had such a loss, and that everybody
is lamenting his death, as if he were a near friend.
I have had quantities of papers and letters from
America, where the grief for that great man seems
to have been wonderfully real, and the funeral
admirable in its simplicity. I don't think any of
the English papers have said that he was buried in

full dress, like Napoleon—a blue coat and white
cravat, waistcoat, trousers, and gloves.   Everett's
speech was very fine ; and so are some of the poems.
They have reprinted my paper on him in almost
every journal in the States.   Love to all.

Ever faithfully yours,

M. R. M.

To Charles Boner

SWALLOWFIELD, *July* 28, 1853.

I have been reading with absorbing interest
Haydon's life.   It is a most painful and most fasci-
nating book, and people who knew far less of him
than I, seem to feel it equally.   It makes Moore's
life, always frivolous, seem rags and tinsel in the
comparison.   Mr. Taylor has done his work admir-
ably, as concerns the living, and as giving a most
characteristic picture of the dead.   But considering
that there were twenty-nine folio volumes of
journals, closely written, ledger-like books, and
that one of the three published octavos is filled with
autobiography distinct from them, it seems to me
he might have omitted the prayers and the bitter
spite against the sitters.   He of course wished to
give a complete portrait, and he has done so.   The
man always reminded me of Benvenuto Cellini,
and the book has the same character.   I had forgotten the sonnet of mine which is included, and
thought, till I saw it, that it was the earlier one
inserted in the Dramatic Scenes.

Did I tell you that on the Thursday before his death, sending some things to be taken care of by Miss Barrett, he sent my portrait (a head cut out of a great picture larger than life, over-coloured but strangely like) as a present ; then called and said he would only leave it as a loan—on Tuesday he killed himself. There is no mention of that episode of my portrait in the book (I dare say Mr. Taylor did not know it), and I cannot tell what has become of it.

I have been seeing a great deal of the Kingsleys lately. Charming people ! He is not the least Alton Lockeish, but a frank, cordial, high-bred gentleman, and she just fit for a poet's wife. Do you know him ? He says that he certainly either knows personally or has heard much of a Charles Boner, a very handsome dark man—living amongst German princes—a great scholar in many ways, and he thought author of *Chamois Hunting*, &c. But then, that Charles Boner was originally of Edinburgh, and had three sisters great beauties, very dashing, and one of them married to some celebrated man. I told him that my friend, to whom the first part of the description applied exactly, was born at Bath, and educated for the most part in Devonshire, and that I had only heard of one excellent sister, whom I believed to be single. It mystified him exceedingly. I let him see what you say of the German poets, and then we talked of Poe.

If you know Charles Kingsley you are not likely

to forget him, for he is a man after your own heart, who would go chamois hunting himself if he could, as manly a creature as ever lived and as gentle and courteous as manly men commonly are. He is seven or eight miles off unluckily, but does not mind it to come here, which is a great comfort to me.

Alfred Tennyson was with him lately, much softened and improved by the birth of his child. They are looking for a house near her friends, but would come here, Mr. Kingsley thinks, if we could find him a habitation. I should like that much. We are expecting Hawthorne every day. He sent me word the day after his landing at Liverpool, and he and his friend Mr. Ticknor (the great publisher of Boston, partner of my friend Mr. Fields) are only waiting dear Mr. Bennoch's leisure to come here with him and his wife. Mr. Ticknor's coming this year keeps dear Mr. Fields in America, but it is only fair that the other should come, and next year, if I be spared, we shall see that beloved friend. I wonder whether Hawthorne will talk or no ! They say that for the most part he is perfectly silent, grave, shy, almost morose, with brilliant but very rare half-hours. Well ! if anybody can bring him out it will be Mr. Bennoch and Mr. Kingsley. They are frankness itself. What a nice letter was the Prince of Leiningen's ! Our Queen's half-brother, is he not ? and how entirely you have earned the pleasure you will enjoy ! It must be very gratifying to find your work so appreciated by those who know best. God bless you, dear friend.

Ever gratefully yours,
M. R. MITFORD.

To the Rev. William Harness, Kensington Gore

SWALLOWFIELD, *Dec.* 7, 1854.

MY VERY DEAR FRIEND,

I am so glad that you agree with me about Fielding. Of course there are good things in *Tom Jones*, such as Partridge's criticism upon Garrick ; but take it for all in all, I know no book so much over-rated. I am now reading *Humphrey Clinker*. How very superior that is ! How much fuller of gaiety ! The one thing that has provoked me is Smollett's pleadings against York Minster. But the characters are capital, and the *laisser aller* perfect. The expedition might have taken place, and the letters might have been written, which is more than one can say for any of Richardson's books, wonderful as Lovelace is—a perfect inspiration, which the prig who wrote it never understood. *That* might have been dictated by some spirit, say of Congreve, only I believe he was not dead. After I have finished *Humphrey Clinker* I shall try *Peregrine Pickle* and *Roderick Random*, and then go to *Gil Blas* and *Don Quixote*. It is a long while since I read *Gil Blas*. This is going the round of the famous comic romances ; but some, not so famous, are much better. I assure you there is no com-

parison between *Tom Jones* and *Hemsprong*, whether
for cleverness or as a matter of mere amusement ;
allowing always for what, sixty years ago, was called
the mad philosophy. Scott thought of it pretty
much as I do.

Just now I have been reading the *feuilletons* of the
Presse, that contain the *Mémoires* of Georges Sand
—very kindly sent to me by Henry Chorley. Bits
are charming, especially some bird stories, which
have great interest for me now, because some weeks
ago a robin tapped at my window, and finding himself supplied—a tray fastened outside the window-
sill for his accommodation, and kept well stored
with bread crumbs for his use—he has not only
been constant in his own visits, but has brought
his friends and kinsfolk, to my great content. Her
love of birds and her skill in taming them was
hereditary, her mother being the daughter of a little
oiseleur upon the Pont Neuf, whilst her father was
a grandson of Marshal Saxe. Is not this a charming
pedigree ? Marshal Saxe being an illegitimate son
of Augustus, King of Poland, it follows that Madame
Sand was amongst the nearest relations of Louis the
Eighteenth and Charles the Tenth—much nearer
than the Orleans branch. Some of the correspondence between her father and her grandmother
is delightful. Of course she has touched it up
—and there are traits of jealous fondness in the old
grandmother's letter, equal to anything in Madame
de Sévigné. Still there is a want of truthfulness
all through. You feel that you are reading a

plaidoyer for the exceptional woman, and not a true narrative of her life—or rather the lives of her ancestors, for as yet she is not born.

What a grievous thing this war is ! And how wretchedly incompetent our miserable Government ! God bless you, dearest friend ! Love to dear Mary.

Ever yours,
M. R. M.